IF ONLY YOU COULD READ MY MIND

A guide to help couples understand each other and connect

by CLARE BOWLES

Published by

Box 28, 1694 Burnstown Road,
Burnstown, Ontario, Canada K0J 1G0
Telephone (613) 432-7697 or 1-800-465-6072

ISBN 1-894263-26-X
Printed and bound in Canada

Cover artwork by Christine Tripp
Layout and Design by Derek McEwen
Printing by Custom Printers of Renfrew Ltd.
General Store Publishing House
Burnstown, Ontario, Canada

Canadian Cataloguing in Publication Data

Bowles, Clare, 1951
If only you could read my mind

Includes bibliographical references.
ISBN 1-894263-26-X

1. Intimacy (Psychology) 2. Typology (Psychology)
I. Title

HQ734.B75 2000 158.2 C00-900797-0

DEDICATION

This book is dedicated to my husband Ian – who I still, occasionally, expect to read my mind.

ACKNOWLEDGEMENTS

I would like to acknowledge the support and encouragement I received while I struggled to complete this book – finishing projects is always difficult for perceptive types!

First of all, I'd like to thank my husband Ian for keeping me going when I became discouraged and for providing the financial support that allowed me to take the time off to write.

I'd also like to thank the following people for the invaluable support they gave me:

Michele MacHattie, Mary Toohey and June Rogers for reading the early drafts and contributing very helpful comments as well as much needed encouragement,

Jane Derrick, my editor, for being in tune with what I wanted to say and giving me her ideas for presenting it better,

Maggie Mamen, who first suggested the idea of writing this book.

Finally, I would like to thank all the couples I have worked with for giving me reason to be optimistic about the future of couples' relationships.

CONTENTS

PREFACE

When I first came to Canada in the early 1980s, I realized, as a new mother with a small baby, that my main focus now would be family life. In many ways, I was very ill equipped to handle this new role. Away from family and friends, my husband was initially my only friend. I became aware of how difficult it was for me to communicate my wishes directly to him. My own learning experiences with handling my new family role led me to look more carefully at the identity/confidence crisis that hits new parents.

Professionally, I made the decision to move from teaching challenging teenagers to counselling adults. While in the process of retraining, and in keeping with my interest in the communication challenges of new parents, I proposed to the local YM/YWCA that I facilitate a support group for new parents. They were not interested in my support group idea, but asked me instead to teach their Assertive Communication course. I did—but long before I was able to assert myself effectively!

Listening to the students in my classes, I soon understood that I was not the only one having difficulty communicating with my partner. I began to see that other very able individuals, while strong and forceful in their careers, also had this same problem at home. I wondered what was going on. Why was it that individuals who were able to express themselves very well in other situations, suddenly became fearful of being direct with the person they most cared for?

As I continued to teach these classes, I noticed that as these same individuals became more assertive in their relationships, they usually ended up getting closer to their partners. The fear that their partners would not accept their new assertive approach appeared to be unfounded.

During this time I went back to school so that I could qualify to work with adults as a counsellor for individuals and couples. Every couple I saw at that time, and almost every couple since, stated that they had difficulty communicating with each other. I began to understand that they would be able to solve their disagreements themselves if they had better communication skills. Teaching these skills thus became my main focus with couples.

Soon after starting to work in private practice, I came across the idea of personality types. I found this whole way of identifying personality traits fascinating, and endeavoured to find out as much as I could about it. I was first introduced to using the personality traits as a team-building tool in the workplace, but soon recognized that an understanding of personality types would be useful for improving communication between couples and to help them understand their differences in an interesting and enjoyable way.

When I ask couples what initially attracted them to each other, they tell me how exciting they found their differences. But after several years of living together, these very differences became a main source of irritation. Why does this happen? From my understanding of the dynamics of couple relationships, it seems that couples enjoy the diversity that another perspective on life gives them and **at the same time** expect that their partners will see things in the same way they do; when they do not, they feel betrayed. This assumption was something they never analyzed or discussed. Often when they talk about this in my office they immediately realize the dissonance in their thinking. The problem was, they never really thought about it before.

My sessions on personality differences are nearly always filled with laughter, as my clients realize they are not unique in their behaviour patterns. The first part of this book examines these personality traits, and I hope will build understanding and an appreciation of the richness they add to your relationship.

Learning how to communicate effectively seems to be a piece of education that is left out of our schooling. When we get married, we are somehow supposed to know how to communicate with the person with whom we have chosen to share our lives. We have to resolve conflicts and differences, listen when we are told things we don't want to hear, and negotiate our way through shared housework, parenting, financial planning, and so on, without any guidance. This is very difficult, especially when some of the strategies we learned as children no longer work. The second part of this book looks at developing the communication skills that I have found useful for couples.

INTRODUCTION

Fairy tales have really deceived us. We all read them as kids and believed that all we had to do was find the right partner and we'd be set up for life. What a disappointment! No one told us what to do when our prince or princess went off in a sulk and wouldn't speak to us for hours; or warned us that leaving the top off the toothpaste tube would cause an outburst of anger. With our perfect companion, we would live "happily ever after" with no effort at all. People are beginning to get the message that this fairy tale ending doesn't describe real relationships, but no one seems to know for sure what to do about it.

For most people these days, finding a partner is not too difficult, but keeping the relationship going through the stresses of child rearing and the heavy demands of the work environment is a real challenge. Many books have been written recently on male and female differences and they have been very helpful. However, there is not much written about the communication skills we need in order to do the hard work of building and maintaining a relationship.

RELATIONSHIPS: FROM PAST TO PRESENT

Relationships are very different now from the way they were in the past. Let's take a look at how relationships have evolved over the past century, and how they have changed to become far more complex and confusing.

At the beginning of the twentieth century, couples were more likely to live "happily ever after"; or at least were not likely to question whether they *were* living happily ever after. Partners in relationships had clear roles that were generally accepted by both parties. In this way, they could become a team that dealt very effectively with the work of providing food for the table, shelter for the family and care for the children. The roles were so well set that in general there was little resentment that they existed and little argument as to how they were carried out. Everybody knew that was the way life was. Each partner had his or her own area of expertise and independently made the ultimate decisions connected to these roles.

For the most part, at that time, couples lived close to their extended families. Women went to their female relatives for advice on child rearing, cooking, and other matters pertaining to the home. For companionship, they generally relied on family and the friends they had known since childhood. Men also relied on their family of origin, usually their fathers, for advice related to work. They would often follow in their fathers' footsteps and would work with their male relatives. They would socialize with the people with whom they worked.

Early in the twentieth century, unless they were part of the small minority of the wealthy, both male and female partners were very busy. The men would work hard all day, and come home to eat and sleep before going off to work again. The women would also work hard raising children and caring for the house; and often would supplement the family income with outside work of their own. Neither partner expected to have meaningful emotional or intellectual communication with the other.

Over the past century, marriages and couple relationships have changed dramatically. There have been huge changes in the status of men and women—changes in the kind of work they do and in the mobility of families. These changes have had quite an impact on family life and on how couples survive in committed relationships.

The First World War set the stage for the emancipation of women. Young men left the farms and factories to go off to war. Considerable numbers of them died. Women were left to fill the gap and began to play a vital part in the economic survival of the country. Women got a taste of financial independence. There was no going back.

Over the next fifty years, education became more accessible to both men and women. For some, physical labour gave way to more intellectual and sedentary work. Labour unions fought for more humane working hours and conditions. People had more leisure time and more energy to enjoy it. Generally people had more money, and couples could survive on one income. They began to enjoy free time together.

For the most part, during this time male and female roles in relationships did not change too much. The men were still providing the income and the women were still responsible for the home and caring for the children. However, women were now more educated and had become less satisfied with their role. More access to education had led to more diverse job opportunities for the male partner, and couples were no longer staying close to home. Women, who had been encouraged to use their brains, found themselves isolated from friends and family with only small children for company. Men felt less secure away from their place of birth and no longer had the support system of the family and co-workers to which they had become accustomed while growing up.

At first, men and women did not question their roles too carefully; perhaps they were afraid to rock a boat that had been stable for centuries. All change is fearful, and changing the balance of marital roles was a colossal undertaking. Women became depressed and were medicated with tranquillizers. Men became depressed and medicated themselves with alcohol. Family life became more isolated for all concerned.

For the next thirty years, couple relationships evolved to try to address these problems. Women went to work and brought another income into the family. They now had much less time to devote to the care of the family and were no longer able to be effective in this role by themselves. They began to look for support from their partners, but had no models to help them know what was reasonable to expect or how to ask for it. Many believed their struggle was obvious and that their partners, though aware, chose to ignore it. Others, without the skills or the confidence to ask for help, continued on their own until they burned out. Still others believed they should be able to do it all, at great cost to their relationships. For whatever the reason, the result was that women in relationships became exhausted because they either could not or would not communicate their needs to their partners.

While women's roles were changing, men were also having a difficult time. What they had been led to expect from marriage was not happening. They were working hard to provide for their families just as their fathers had done and could not understand what was wrong with their wives. They might understand their wives' wish to work, but it was not a necessity; in the early stages of this evolution, couples could still survive on one salary. Men felt abandoned. There might not be a meal ready when they got home, their clothes were no longer ironed promptly or at all and, probably most serious of all, their partners were too exhausted for a sexual relationship and even resented their husbands for expecting one. Men, just like their wives, had no models for dealing with this situation and no family to consult. They felt hurt and unloved, but had no skills to communicate these feelings. Their most likely strategy was to withdraw and work even harder in an effort to regain their mate's love and approval.

The next stage in this tragedy has more to do with external changes. In the world of work, the computer age arrived. Corporate communication became faster and faster, and the competition between companies for development of new products and the share of the market became vicious. Consumers had more money to spend and there were so many more things to spend it on. Credit cards became common and couples began getting into debt. Again there were no models to help couples communicate about this. Finances were clear-cut in the past. There had been no opportunities for getting seriously into debt for the average person and generally only one member of the partnership had taken responsibility for how money was spent. Previously, there was little money left over for leisure activities—nor had the couple the energy to take part in them—so differences of opinion in this realm were rare. In the evolving couple relationship, as women became more interested in handling family finances, dealing with money became an area of conflict and nobody knew how to address the issue constructively.

The last act in this drama relates to the increase in both the cost of living and the debt load of couples. For many, it is no longer a choice that they both work—they now expect to own their own home and have all the modern conveniences. There is now more competition for education, so children need to be stimulated as early and as much as possible for them to be able to compete successfully for university places and the shrinking job market. All this costs more and more money and therefore requires more and more work to earn that money. Husbands and wives are now both working full-time jobs. They work more overtime than ever so as to make enough money to keep up their standard of living and secure their jobs. They have virtually no opportunities to spend time together. If they can find the time, they certainly don't want to spoil it by addressing all the issues that are mentioned above. Therefore, they remain unresolved.

The main belief was, and still is, that to confront such issues would end up destroying a relationship. No one had the skills to address these concerns in a constructive, non-threatening way.

Now that we have explored the historical context of the evolution of marriage, we can examine the skills we need to handle the changing roles and added stresses of a relationship in today's world.

WHAT SKILLS DO WE NEED TO LEARN?

When couples try to communicate with each other, even the most basic messages can be misconstrued. Information that seems to be clearly articulated is interpreted completely differently from what was meant. How does this happen? An attempt at answering this question will be the main focus of this book.

For communication between two people to be effective, two separate roles are required: a speaker and a listener. This may seem obvious, but very often in couples there may be two speakers, two listeners, or even two individuals who believe loving couples should be able to read each other's minds.

When communication fails and partners are hurt or disappointed, there may be difficulties in speaking clearly and assertively; or there may be blocks at the listening end.

COMMUNICATING AS A SPEAKER

First, let's look at what can happen to prevent the *speaker* from being effective. In the following chapters we will examine these areas more closely.

CLARITY

Individuals appear to have been taught from early childhood never to be direct. When I want something, especially for myself, then I am being selfish and had better cloak it in terms that avoid making me seem self-centred. This clouding of my self-interest can very efficiently obliterate all clarity in my message.

An example of such communication is, "Some couples go out on Friday nights," meaning, "I'd like us to go out on Friday nights." The first statement is just information about how other couples behave and, though it may be interesting to your partner, contains no requirement for action. The second is a clear statement of what you want to do, and though it still may be misinterpreted, it won't be because of lack of clarity.

BODY LANGUAGE

Normally when we communicate, about 90% of our communication is in our body language. However, in relationships, the way we give messages with our bodies is far more complex than when we communicate with strangers. If I scowl at my partner while saying, "I really like your new haircut," he/she might decide that the comment was insincere because of the body language. However, for reasons mentioned later (under "Be Congruent," in Chapter 6), in couples, body language may often *prevent* the right message from getting across, and the actual words provide the true meaning.

Unfortunately, in couple relationships, the more hostile and angry we look, the more desperate we are for a loving hug. We don't realize that only a very determined warrior would dare to pass through the barrier we have presented. Also, the natural human response when attacked is to fight back or withdraw. This fight or flight response to perceived danger is Stone Age in origin and does not pay attention to the rational part of our brains which say, "Hey, he/she is just feeling hurt and needs a little comfort!"

When you communicate, if your body language is hostile or ambiguous, you will usually not be satisfied with the response you get. Instead of closeness, you will get withdrawal. Instead of problem solving, you will get a fight.

DELIBERATE DISTORTIONS

Many times in relationships we deliberately distort the message we want to convey. We might say,

"I notice there's a good play on this week, but you probably wouldn't want to go."

When we mean,

"I'd like to see Hamlet. It's playing at the local theatre."

We usually do this because we are afraid and want to protect either our partner or ourselves from hurt or disagreement. We may be sensitive to our partner's feelings and not want to say outright something that may hurt; or we may be afraid for ourselves, feeling that being too direct might make us vulnerable to rejection or an angry response. Although we are not direct, we do expect our partner to get the message anyway.

COMMUNICATING AS A LISTENER

Next, let's look at what happens from the listener's end that may stop the message from getting across as meant. We will look at listening skills in more detail later in the book.

EXPECTATIONS AND ASSUMPTIONS

What we are expecting to hear plays a key part in how we perceive messages. If I already feel guilty, I will hear criticism in my partner's comments. Sometimes expectations conform to your own history from your family of origin. For example, if you were blamed for everything that went wrong in the family when you were a kid, with statements such as, "Now you've made your mother cry!" or "Look, you made me drop the dinner dishes!" you may well grow up feeling omnipotent. That is, if anything goes wrong, it has to be your fault. If you feel that way, even a simple statement like, "It's raining outside" will prompt you to apologize. You are likely to see criticism even when it may not be there.

MINDSET

Most couples, at one time or another, equate a different viewpoint with betrayal or lack of love. When you think this way you may often hear agreement or at least compliance, even when it doesn't exist. You might for instance interpret "maybe" to mean "yes." This holds especially when your partner also believes that couples should think alike and makes his/her message indirect or deliberately distorted.

Sometimes when we hear a message that seems to us clearly to challenge this mindset that couples should think alike, we panic and completely shut down without listening to the whole statement.

FAMILY HISTORY

All the unfinished business from our families of origin can interfere with our ability to hear messages objectively. This is probably the biggest factor that makes it so much more difficult for couples to communicate with one another than with a stranger. How our parents communicated with each other and with us laid down the foundations of our own skills. This, in turn, was influenced by the culture of the time. When we observe very small children, we notice that they state their needs assertively and listen well; for them, these skills have not yet been damaged by cultural standards. As we've grown up we've forgotten how to do this. It is very hard to let go of the values and beliefs we were taught as we neared adulthood. Examples of these beliefs are, "Women shouldn't disagree," and "Men shouldn't express their feelings."

DIFFERENT INTERPRETATIONS OF MEANING

When people join in a relationship, they come from different worlds. Their understanding of the meanings of words and phrases can be completely different. Unfortunately it can take years and sometimes a period of couple counselling for these differences to come to light. We just assume that our understanding is right and we see no need to question it. This can even happen when messages are stated directly and assertively. For example, a husband expressed to his wife that he felt quite angry over something she had done. She became very distressed about this, withdrew, and considered leaving her marriage. It turned out that for this woman anger meant physical violence, and what she heard was that her husband was threatening to hit her. He had no idea of the impact of his statement.

SO WHAT'S THIS BOOK ABOUT?

In this book I will look at why misunderstandings can easily occur, teach skills/rules that will be useful for communicating in an effective, non-confronting fashion, and describe typical situations in which you can use these skills. I will start by examining the personality differences that can cause misunderstandings. I will follow this by describing various skills and techniques that enable clearer communication and better listening. I will end by discussing typical areas of difficulty in couples. To illustrate the different styles and skills I will be demonstrating, I will use a number of fictional couples. A cast of characters is listed at the beginning of the next chapter along with their personality types. These personality types will be explained in full detail in the chapters following.

In the remainder of this book, I have provided quite a few techniques. It is not necessary to apply all of them, all the time; couples tend to be quite forgiving of one another as long as they are convinced there is love and caring in the relationship. The purpose of this book is to empower couples to take charge of their communication difficulties and to recognize that "happily ever after" requires hard but worthwhile effort!

CAST OF CHARACTERS

Annie	– extroverted, intuitive, feeling and perceptive (ENFP)
Bob	– introverted, sensing, thinking and judging (ISTJ)
Cathy	– extroverted, intuitive, feeling and judging (ENFJ)
Dave	– introverted, sensing, thinking and perceptive (ISTP)
Ed	– extroverted, sensing, thinking and judging (ESTJ)
Fran	– introverted, intuitive, feeling and perceptive (INFP)
Greg	– introverted, feeling and judging (IFJ)
Helen	– introverted, thinking and judging (ITJ)
Iris	– sensing, thinking and judging (STJ)
John	– intuitive, thinking and perceptive (NTP)
Karen	– intuitive judge (NJ)
Leo	– sensing perceptive (SP)

I = Introvert	S = Sensing	T = Thinking	J = Judging
E = Extrovert	N = Intuitive	F = Feeling	P = Perceiving

As you will notice, I have not given complete personality types for all the characters—I felt it would be too complex, given the focus of this book. I have featured the personality traits that were important to illustrate the examples I have given. In most cases I have isolated particular characteristics rather than dealing with the combination of the four traits.

For most of my examples, I have used Annie and Bob. These two are at opposite ends of the personality spectrum. Ed and Fran, and Cathy and Dave, are also opposites and will come up frequently to illustrate personality and communication differences.

Chapter 1

Am I an Introvert or an Extrovert?

One aspect of couple relationships that influences the way they interact with each other is their personalities. People with different personalities communicate in different ways and this causes a huge amount of confusion, especially if we assume that our partners communicate in the same way we do. In the next few chapters, I will examine these differences in personality.

Introverts and extroverts have very different styles of communication, causing much confusion in relationships.

Extroverts' main area of interest is the outside world. When they have an idea or an opinion, their first urge is to share it with others. They do not necessarily use other people's ideas—although they may certainly be open to them—but are energized by others in their thinking and decision-making.

Extroverts:

- think out loud, drawing energy from the company of others

- share their thoughts quite forcefully but may change their minds as they speak
- recharge their energy in the company of people
- respond quickly to others, sometimes before others have finished speaking
- do not leave much of a gap between sentences or thoughts
- often enjoy distractions and don't usually mind being interrupted in tasks
- can focus on many things at once
- may enjoy the company of many people at once
- speak without planning exactly what they are going to say

If most of the above apply to you, then you are probably an extrovert (E).

Introverts' main area of interest is the inner world. When they have an idea or an opinion, their first urge is to develop it by themselves using their own inner energy. They are energized in thinking and decision-making by their own resources. They are generally uncomfortable sharing their ideas until they are well formed and often may not share them at all. Unlike extroverts, who believe that people will be delighted to hear their point of view, introverts do not expect others to be interested in what they have to say.

Introverts:

- think things through by themselves and do not always share their thoughts
- share their thoughts quite tentatively and do not easily change their minds
- recharge their energy by themselves
- are slow to respond—they do not like being put on the spot
- leave gaps between their sentences
- do not enjoy distractions and are not comfortable with being interrupted in tasks

- like to focus on one thing at a time and are not quick to switch focus
- prefer the company of one other person or two or three if they know them really well
- usually rehearse what they are going to say unless they are very comfortable with the listener

If most of the above apply to you, then you are probably an introvert (I).

Extroverts and introverts often share a relationship. On the positive side, these two types can create a useful balance between the external and internal world. Extroverts like to talk and introverts like to listen. Introverts slow extroverts down when they are moving too fast, and extroverts speed introverts up when they are moving too slowly. However, these two personality types could confuse each other. I will focus now on this confusion and some ideas on how to work through it. In the examples, Annie is an extrovert and Bob is introverted.

AT THE END OF THE WORKING DAY

Extroverts and introverts recharge their batteries at the end of a stressful day in very different ways. Annie, the extrovert, will come home eager to share the day with Bob. She will not feel comfortable until she has talked about all that has happened. If there has been some unpleasantness, she will need to verbalize the experience before she can put it away and carry on with her day. On the other hand, Bob, the introvert, will come home eager to find some peace and quiet so he can mull over his day internally. He will have little desire to share the difficult moments of his day, especially before they have been properly processed.

As you can see, and are probably experiencing if you are an introvert/extrovert couple, this contrast in needs can make the end of the working day very difficult. The difficulty is exacerbated if the extrovert has had a very introverted working day, such as looking after a small baby or sitting in front of a computer; or the introvert has had a very extroverted day, for example as a teacher or salesperson. The most effective way I have found of dealing with this difference is for couples to negotiate their talking and quiet time and for these times to be respected. When Bob, the introvert, is behind a newspaper, he is taking his "recharge" time. If he is constantly interrupted, then that time will last all night. Similarly, if Annie, the extrovert, gets no attention when unloading her day, then she will talk all night or withdraw with resentment.

I often hear from couples that they can respect their decisions for quiet and talking times, but the kids don't pay any attention. Children can be taught to respect a quiet time too. It can be during the time of their favourite TV program or their homework. If they want attention during that time—unless it's an emergency—they can learn to wait.

DIFFERENT STYLES OF SHARING IDEAS

Extroverts and introverts share their ideas in very different ways. Annie, as the extrovert, will share an idea or decision with enthusiasm and force, even when it is still on the drawing board. This can sound to Bob, the introvert, as if Annie has really made a decision. Often Annie's decision will be followed by a request for an immediate opinion from Bob. This puts Bob on the spot. He hasn't had a chance to process the information yet but feels pressure to respond. He will often simply say "no"—to him, the safest response, given the lack of time:

Annie: Kate's on the phone. Her dog just had puppies. The kids have always wanted a puppy. She wants to know if we'll have one?

Bob: No!

In this case, Bob had no time to process the request. Kate was on the phone and waiting for an answer. The consequences of a "yes" here are far-reaching and haven't been discussed. Because Bob was put on the spot, his response was far stronger than he might have meant it to be and may have blocked future discussions, perhaps to the disappointment of both of them. In this kind of situation, the following interaction will work better:

Annie: Kate was just on the phone. Her dog's just had puppies and she's asking whether we want one. What do you think about owning a dog? I know the kids would love one.

Bob: I'm not sure. I'd like to think about it for a bit.

Annie: She needs to know fairly quickly, as there are other people who want one. How about we call her back tomorrow?

Bob: Sure.

In another similar situation, Annie may come up with an idea that doesn't have any long-term effect. In this instance, Bob may decide to agree even though he hasn't had a chance to think about it:

Annie: Let's go out for a Chinese meal tonight.

Bob: Okay.

In this case, they may both go out for a meal that neither of them wants. When Annie voiced her original idea, it was supposed to be the beginning of a discussion about where to eat. Remember, Annie thinks out loud. As soon as she had spoken, she remembered that she'd had indigestion after eating at the only good Chinese restaurant in town, and that Chinese food doesn't agree with her at the moment. Bob would prefer to grab a burger and go to a movie but he doesn't care that much either way, so he goes along with Annie. Underneath he wishes Annie were less controlling and that they could do what he wanted for a change. Annie feels frustrated that they couldn't have a discussion about where to go. Why do decisions always have to be made so quickly? A simple way around this problem is for Annie to ask Bob for his opinion. Introverts like to be invited to give their opinion with an open-ended question—one that does not require a yes or no answer:

Annie: I'd like to go out for a Chinese meal tonight. What would you like to do?

Bob: We could do that. But I think I'd prefer to grab a burger and watch a movie. There's a good selection of movies on at the moment.

Annie: That's a good idea. I've just remembered that Chinese food isn't agreeing with me just now anyway. How about we go and see . . .?

When Bob, the introvert, comes up with an idea, completely different rules apply. Before Bob suggests something, he will have thought it through, and if he gets to share his idea then he is usually pretty committed to it. However, he will not share it with Annie's enthusiasm. His approach will be far more tentative. Unfortunately, this appearance of uncertainty fools Annie into believing that Bob is not serious about his idea and she responds to it as if it were the beginning of a discussion:

Bob: I was thinking about us going to see my mom at the end of the month.

Annie: Okay. But I don't have time this month. I'm supposed to be helping Kate choose patterns for her curtains and I said I'd go out with friends from work next weekend and I've got a work project to finish. How about the middle of next month?

Bob: How come everyone else comes before me?

In this case, Annie responded to Bob's initial statement as if he were an extrovert and Bob felt rejected that his idea wasn't treated with more respect. Bob may want to start by being more direct. If this doesn't work, then he will need to emphasize the importance of his wish:

Bob: I'd like us to visit my mom at the end of the month.

Annie: Okay. But I don't have time this month. I'm supposed to be helping Kate choose patterns for her curtains and I said I'd go out with friends from work next weekend and I've got a work project to finish. How about the middle of next month?

Bob: That won't work. I really want to go two weeks from now, because Greg's going to be there and I haven't seen him in ages. Can't you reschedule some of your plans?

Annie: Why didn't you say so to start with? The work thing's not important and Kate can wait. I'll finish my project this weekend and we can go.

DIFFERENCE IN FOCUS

Extroverts are able to focus on many different things at the same time. Those of us who have extroverted teenagers have seen them watch TV, do their homework and talk on the phone simultaneously. (This ability seems at its most advanced during the teenage years!) Because of this, extroverts are able to switch attention quickly and often welcome an interruption. Introverts are quite different. They like to focus on one thing at a time and that will include silently sitting and thinking. They do not welcome interruptions and in fact can be quite irritated by them. If Annie wants Bob's attention, she may need to grab it first before she speaks. Otherwise, the beginning of her sentence will not be heard and its meaning lost:

Annie: I'm going up to the mall. Do you want to come?

Bob: (irritated) Where do you want me to go?

Annie: To the mall . . . weren't you listening?

Bob: (even more irritated) No, I wasn't. I was trying to read my book.

If this is a problem, such questions as "Have you got a moment?" or "Can I ask you something?" or "Could I interrupt you for a minute?" can be useful.

Annie: Can I interrupt you for a moment?

Bob: Okay . . .

Annie: I'm going to the mall. Do you want to come?

Bob: No thanks, I want to finish this book. I'm just getting to an interesting bit.

QUESTIONS

Extroverts and introverts respond quite differently to questions. Annie, the extrovert, enjoys questions. She sees them as continuing a conversation and is delighted to answer them. Bob, on the other hand, often sees questions as doubting his integrity. When questioned, he does not hear the message, "I'd like to hear more about this," but hears instead messages such as, "You don't know what you're talking about," or "Your thinking is muddled." He might become frustrated that the whole of his message is not completely understood the first time and take that as a failure on his own or Annie's part. Bob may well forget that Annie has not been party to all the internal processing that led up to his thought; or he may just wish that he did not have to repeat the whole process for her.

There are two ways around this. Bob can change his expectation that Annie should be able immediately to grasp what he is saying. He will then be able to interpret her question as clarifying the issue for her own better understanding. Alternatively, he can share his thinking earlier so that Annie is more involved in the development of the idea. Both of these will take effort on Bob's part. Annie could also reassure Bob that she is not questioning his thinking, but just seeking clarification:

Bob: I'm thinking of getting a new car radio.

Annie: What made you decide to get a new car radio? I'm just interested.

Bob: Well, my speakers don't seem to be working well and it would be as cheap to buy a new radio as to try and fix them.

Rather than,

Bob: I'm thinking of getting a new car radio.

Annie: Why do you want a new car radio?

Bob: . . . (silence).

LISTENING

Extroverts and introverts listen in different ways. Bob, the introvert, leaves gaps between his sentences when he is speaking so that he can formulate his next sentence. Annie, who never leaves gaps, assumes that he must have finished speaking and jumps in with her response. Often when I'm working with a couple, I hear, "He/she never talks to me," followed by, "He/she never listens to what I have to say," from the other partner. This is usually because the introverted partner has become irritated with the constant interruptions and has ceased bothering to speak at all:

Bob: I'm thinking about not taking any contracts this summer . . .

Annie: Well that's great for you. I wish I could sit around and do nothing all summer!

Bob: I didn't say I was going to do nothing all summer. Why don't you listen?

This problem can be solved if Annie gives Bob the chance to continue. Alternatively, Bob, when he is interrupted, can let Annie know he hasn't finished speaking:

Bob: I'm thinking about not taking any contracts this summer . . .

Annie: You don't want to take any contracts this summer . . . and? (Annie is careful to sound supportive rather than impatient here.)

Or,

Bob: I'm thinking about not taking any contracts this summer . . .

Annie: Well that's great . . .

Bob: (interrupting) I'm not finished. . . . There's a course I want to take over the summer. It looks really good . . . just what I've been looking for.

This is easier to do if you can recognize that the difficulty is caused by a difference in communication style rather than disrespect.

Annie, as the extrovert, enjoys speaking. Often when Bob is talking she is formulating what she's going to say next. This may prevent her from hearing Bob's message accurately. She may listen only to the first sentence and then start thinking about her reply. Bob, being more tentative in his communication, often leaves the meat of his message to the end and this is therefore lost on Annie. When Annie responds in a way that seems off-topic, Bob gives up and wonders why he bothers. If you are the extroverted partner, listen to the end. You will have no difficulty thinking of something to say when the time comes. If you are getting too much information at once and can't take it all in, then use paraphrasing in the gaps provided by the introvert. If you are the introverted partner, you may need to repeat what was not heard rather than give up and feel resentful:

Bob: I was thinking of taking a holiday the first two weeks of July . . . I know we'd agreed on the last two weeks of August, but it turns out a guy at work has an apartment in California that's free those two weeks and he's offered it to us for practically nothing.

Annie: I thought we'd agreed on August. You're always changing your mind. We'll never find anywhere to go at this short notice.

Bob: You didn't hear the last part of what I said. I said we've been offered an apartment in California for virtually nothing. All we've got to do is see if we can get a reasonable flight.

Bob, as the introvert, is usually better at listening. The difficulty here is that he rarely shows that he is doing so. He will often listen and take in the information in silence, which is frustrating for Annie, who would dearly love some feedback:

Annie: I'm so frustrated. I came home expecting to finish this paper I've been working on and it seems I've left the whole lot at work.

Bob: . . . (silence)

What happens here is that Bob can't figure out what to say—either to solve the problem or to comfort Annie—so he remains silent. He has heard all the content; he just isn't sure how to reply and it may take him a while to figure it out. In the meantime, Annie feels rejected and ignored. This type of misunderstanding is often seen as caused by a male/female difference. Introverted women do tend to listen more actively, giving verbal feedback, because they are generally more socially conditioned. However, this is not always so. Female introverts often respond in the same way as Bob. The solution to this problem is easy and is explored more fully in the chapter on listening. All Bob needs to do here is paraphrase what he is hearing and support her distress:

Annie: I'm so frustrated. I came home expecting to finish this paper I've been working on and it seems I've left the whole lot at work.

Bob: You've left all the stuff you need to finish your paper at work? I'd find that really frustrating too!

Bob may also feel overwhelmed with the amount of information coming at him all at once. Annie does not leave gaps between her thoughts so Bob has no time to process them. He may need either to slow her down or interrupt, to ensure that he has understood what she is saying so far.

THE SPEED WITH WHICH IDEAS ARE SHARED

As mentioned in the beginning of this chapter, introverts share their ideas much later than do extroverts. This means that introverts are strongly attached to their ideas when they do eventually get to share them. Because they have thought at great length, and weighed the pros and cons and all possible outcomes and consequences, it can be quite difficult to change their minds.

Bob is quite fearful of sharing his idea with Annie before it is well thought out; he is naturally concerned that Annie may jump on his idea and change it before he has all his arguments in place. The result is that Bob may share a thought or decision on something that concerns both of them very late in his thinking process. The most extreme case I have come across was an introverted wife who came home one day and announced to her husband that she had finally found their new home. Her husband had no idea that she was looking for a house, or even that she was dissatisfied with the house they were living in. Naturally he felt quite hurt and left out.

If you and your mate often find yourselves in a similar situation, each of you can adapt your natural response. As an introvert, you can share your idea earlier, stating that you are not finished in your thinking and certainly not ready to act on it yet; and you can be open to your partner's ideas without feeling you have to act on them. As an extrovert, you can be careful not to jump on an idea and you can avoid pressuring your partner to act on it.

ASKING FOR AN OPINION

When extroverts and introverts ask for an opinion they are in the middle of two completely different processes. When Annie asks for an opinion she may be just beginning her thinking process. Or—and this is most often the case—she may be trying to begin a conversation with Bob. In the former case, Bob's answer may cease to be relevant when Annie has thought some more about it. Bob, not understanding Annie's process, may feel hurt that his opinion is not valued. This is especially so if Annie has then gone on to consult with others as she continues to develop her thought, and ends up following someone else's advice.

However, if Annie is beginning a conversation, then once she gets an answer from Bob, she may try again on another topic or even the same topic worded differently. Annie's goal here is not specifically to get Bob's opinion, but simply to have a conversation or a verbal connection with him. Bob, wondering why he is being bombarded with all these questions, becomes irritated or confused. Why does he have to answer that question again? How does this question follow that one? Where's the link? In Bob's mind, he was asked a question and he answered it. What more is there to say?

When Bob, the introvert, asks Annie for her opinion, he has already considered his thought well before consulting with her. When he asks for her opinion, it is to confirm his own thinking or to find out if he has missed anything significant. He is looking for input on his idea rather than beginning a conversation. He my feel quite put out if Annie treats the question as the beginning of a conversation and gives advice that is not well thought out just to continue the interaction. However, from Annie's point of view, if she says nothing, the valuable opportunity for socializing is wasted.

You may find that, although you relate best to an introverted style, you do also enjoy opportunities for conversation just for the sake of interaction. On the other hand, as an extrovert, you may not be particularly excited by conversation with no purpose. This is because the introverted/extroverted style may be modified by the feeling/thinking style. I will discuss this topic later.

IN SUMMARY

So let's look at what we've got so far:

- Introverts recharge their batteries by retreating within in silence while extroverts recharge by talking about their experiences with their partners.
- Extroverts share their thoughts with energy and enthusiasm, even if they have not yet finished processing

them. Introverts share their thoughts with more reserve, even though they are quite decided.

- An extrovert's first idea may not be based on careful thought; an introvert's probably will be.
- Introverts do not like to be put on the spot, and if they are, they will not give their best response. Extroverts can nearly always think of something to say, although they may change their minds later. Therefore, for both personality types, on-the-spot answers are not necessarily indicative of what they really think.
- Introverts leave gaps in their sentences. This does not mean they have finished speaking. Extroverts do not leave gaps and may overwhelm their introverted partners with all the information they relay with no breaks.
- When introverts are silent and don't respond, it does not mean that they are not listening. When extroverts are active and do respond it does not mean that they are listening (they may be thinking of more things to say to keep the conversation going).
- Extroverts share their ideas the minute they think of them. Introverts share their ideas, if at all, when they have come up with a firm statement. This may take a long time.
- Introverts take a few seconds to switch focus from one stimulus to another. Extroverts can focus on many things at once.
- Extroverts perceive questions as a welcome opportunity to have a conversation. Introverts perceive questions as a possible challenge to their thinking and/or integrity. Introverts ask questions to get answers.
- Introverts ask for advice when they have almost completely made up their minds. Extroverts ask for advice at any time during the process of making up their minds. For extroverts, making up their minds is seen as an opportunity for a lot of social interaction.

As you can see, extroverts and introverts have very different styles of communicating. For the most part, although we can adapt a bit, these styles will always exist and need to be respected. If we continue to expect that our relationships can only work if we both respond in the same way, then we will never be satisfied. You will find it is far more constructive to respect the differences between you and your partner and enjoy the balance these styles offer.

A WORD OF CAUTION

Often introverts behave like extroverts. In our culture there are many more extroverts than introverts, and this leads some introverts to cross over in order to get along with the majority. These individuals, when comfortable in their home environment or after a few years in a stable relationship, may revert to being more introverted. Also, they may appear to be the life and soul of the party when out socially and then very quiet in the home environment. Their partners sometimes interpret this change as withdrawal from the relationship and feel rejected. If this has happened to you, check to find out what is going on before you make that assumption.

Chapter 2

Am I Organized or Flexible?

Two individuals who can constantly frustrate each other are the decisive, planning type and the flexible, free-flow type, and they often end up together as partners in a long-term relationship. Their attraction isn't surprising. Their combination creates a good balance of planning and spontaneity, decision and open-mindedness, work and play. However, I have found that these two find it difficult to respect their differences and can often be quite insulting of each other's style.

The decisive personalities—usually called **judging types** (I will use this term for continuity in case you want to look further into this)—routinely move from one decision to another.

Judging types:

- enjoy making decisions
- feel relieved and satisfied when a decision is made
- enjoy planning and scheduling events and the projects that go along with that
- like to know when they are going to do something so they can plan for it

- like to stick to that plan
- will often finish a task ahead of time and enjoy a sense of accomplishment
- generally enjoy some routine
- are stressed when decisions are left unmade
- will argue their point strongly even if it creates conflict in the relationship (this is true especially of extroverted judging types, with their need for quick decisions)

If most of the above applies to you then you are probably a judging type (J).

The flexible personalities—**perceptive types**—observe the world around them and collect data. They have no urge to organize these data as do the judging types, but are content to absorb the knowledge and enjoy it.

Perceptive types:

- like to leave their lives open to spontaneity
- resist planning and schedules
- leave decisions and acting on decisions to the last moment just in case there might be more data to consider
- are uncomfortable with plans made ahead of time
- feel trapped with too many scheduled activities
- enjoy the figuring out process more than making decisions
- are stressed by having to make decisions too quickly
- will often have second thoughts about the decisions they have made
- can be quite confrontational in debate or discussion involving impersonal matters
- prefer to be flexible in their personal relationships and not rock the boat

If most of the above apply to you, then you are probably a perceptive type (P).

As you can see, these two personalities have very separate agendas. While introverted/extroverted types confuse each other, judging/perceptive types often irritate and annoy each other.

The first thing to remember, if you have this balance of judging and perception in your relationship, is that you chose your partner and there must be a part of you that needs and appreciates the gifts offered by this dynamic.

The second thing to remember is that you would still be having difficulties if you were both the same type. Two judging types together are both decisive and like to plan. This is fine if they have both made the same decision and have planned the same way of going about it. If they haven't then they will have a power struggle and both will be equally stressed and distressed when a decision can't be made. Two perceptive types together like to leave things open. In this relationship, decisions are rarely made and things don't get done. In today's busy world, this may mean that there is no time planned for the play activities they both enjoy. They may also act spontaneously by themselves if their partners aren't free to join them.

To illustrate interactions I will introduce a new couple, Cathy and Dave. Cathy is judging and Dave is perceptive. Obviously extroversion and introversion also affect the way these styles are expressed, but we won't worry about that for the moment.

IS A DECISION MADE OR NOT?

Judging types are often frustrated when decisions they think have been made aren't carried out. Perceptive types become frustrated when they share ideas and find that they are acted on as if they are decisions. When Dave suggests they might go out together for a meal on Friday night, he is surprised when, the following day, he hears that a restaurant has been booked. His suggestion was an idea, not a decision. When Cathy suggests they go out for a meal on Friday night, she is surprised when, the following day, she discovers that Dave has arranged a squash game for that night. Her suggestion was a decision, not an idea. These types of situations can cause a fair amount of hurt and distress between couples. To avoid this situation, you need to check what you hear, based on your understanding of your partner's personality:

Dave: I'd like us to go out for dinner on Friday night.

Cathy: Are you committed to that? Shall I book a restaurant?

Dave: No, I'm not sure yet. I'm supposed to be playing squash with Bob but he's not sure he can get a sitter.

Or,

Cathy: I'd like us to go out for dinner on Friday night.

Dave: Let me know when you decide. I might want to play squash.

Cathy: I am decided. Shall I put it on the calendar, or do you want to think about it?

Dave: No, that's fine. Put it in big letters on the calendar.

When you check out your understanding, you can ensure that you are both in tune and you will be less likely to act without consensus.

WHO IS IN CONTROL OF THE DECISION-MAKING?

When perceptive and judging types are together in a relationship, they often feel that the other is controlling them. The perceptive partner thinks the judging partner is in control because he/she is always making decisions and wanting them carried out. The judging ones think the perceptive ones are in control because they resist acting on the decision until they are ready. The way forward here is to find a middle position that is not too stressful for either one:

Cathy: I'd like us to go out for dinner on Friday night.

Dave: Let me know when you decide. I might want to play squash.

Cathy: I am decided. Shall I put it on the calendar, or do you want to think about it?

Dave: I'd like to think about it.

Cathy: When can you let me know?

Dave: How about Friday morning? (When asked, the perceptive type will go as near the deadline as possible.)

Cathy: Today is Monday. I'd like to know by Wednesday lunchtime whether you're coming. That will give me time to plan something else if you're not.

Dave: Okay.

Compromise is the key here. Perceptive types work better with a deadline and judging types are comforted by the knowledge that a decision will be made by a certain time.

Occasionally, when both partners are perceptive, all the decision-making is allocated to one of them—usually the more extroverted of the two. Continual decision-making can be very stressful for a perceptive type and this will cause difficulty for the relationship over time.

SHOPPING

Judging types go shopping with a purpose. They have decided what they want, and when they have found something suitable, they will buy it. Not so their perceptive partners, who go shopping to see what the stores have to offer. They will be very uncomfortable buying anything until they have looked in all the stores and compared looks and prices.

Cathy and Dave are looking for new sofas for the living room. They have neutral colours in the living room and both are agreed that they are looking for a sofa and a love seat in a bold colour. In the first store, they see a set in a deep blue that's on special:

Cathy: We'll have that. It's a great colour and it's on special, too.

Dave: We've only just started looking. We might find a nicer design. And how do we know it's a great price? We've only been in one store.

Cathy: Why do we need to look any further when this is exactly what we want?

Dave: How do we know that we'll like this best until we've seen them all?

In this case it is probably useful for Cathy to listen to Dave. Judging personalities have a tendency to make quick decisions without all the data and often regret them later. After they have gone through a respectable period of data gathering:

Cathy: We've looked in all the stores now and I think we're both agreed that the blue-green set we saw was the most comfortable, nicest colour and best design. Let's buy it.

Dave: I'm not sure. We haven't looked at all the catalogues and we're going to visit my mom next week. Maybe we should look there, too.

At this point it is time for Dave to listen to Cathy. Perceptive personalities do not like to make decisions and will put off making them for as long as they can.

HOLIDAYS

Holidays can be very stressful for this type combination, right from the very start. Cathy, the judging type, likes to plan her holiday well in advance. In January she is already thinking about the summer holidays: when they should take time off, where they should go, and with whom they should book. As far as Dave is concerned, this is far too early for him to be thinking about summer; it's the middle of winter and impossible to imagine what he might want to do when it's warm again. His focus is on the possibility of skiing this weekend. For Cathy, persuading Dave to take her holiday planning seriously is an undertaking fraught with frustration. At this point, it may be to Cathy's advantage to find out what the deadline might be to get a good choice of flights or accommodation.

The next stumbling block is the type of holiday. Cathy will often enjoy holidays with a lot of planned excursions and specific places to visit. This may mean booking tours or including a city where there are sights to see and museums or galleries to visit. She is on holiday and wants to get the very most out of the area she is visiting. Dave, on the other hand, likes to go with the flow. His preference is to get somewhere and then decide what he will do. He likes lots of variety, with chances for play and relaxation. He may not be interested in tourist attractions and may feel restricted by guidebooks, preferring to find out things by himself. He is on holiday and doesn't want to make decisions.

The secret of dealing with all this is again the art of compromise. For a holiday to be successful for both Cathy and Dave, they need to consider a balance of both their needs. This may mean that some time is scheduled for sight-seeing, and some time is also set aside for play, relaxation, or sporting activities. It is important that both Cathy and Dave be assertive regarding their needs and that both take responsibility for the eventual outcome. What sometimes happens is that the perceptive type goes along with the judging type, and then complains when the holiday is not enjoyable.

DEALING WITH CONFLICT

Judging types, especially extroverted judges, can be quite impatient regarding making and carrying out decisions. As stated already, they are stressed by unfinished business and therefore work hard to have everything decided quickly. On the other hand, perceptive personalities, especially introverts, are very uncomfortable committing themselves to decisions. They prefer to make a decision close to the last minute and only when they have weighed all the options.

These two styles often have difficulty dealing with conflict. Judging types, with their impatience to resolve an issue, can be quite forceful if not intimidating at times. Perceptive types, with their need to delay decisions and avoid conflict, find themselves in a difficult situation. They can agree in order to avoid conflict, but then are uncomfortable with their premature commitment. They can, alternatively, resist agreeing in order to avoid premature commitment, but then have to deal with conflict. What the perceptive partner often does in this situation is to agree with the decision and then either not act on it or somehow sabotage the outcome.

For example, Cathy has informed Dave that she wants to have friends over for dinner next Saturday night. Dave is not yet sure what he wants to do on Saturday night, and requests time to think about it. Cathy points out that it's only a week away and feels they should give their friends at least that much notice. Dave can't think of an adequate argument for his position, as he's not sure what he wants to do, so he reluctantly agrees. As the time for the dinner party approaches, Cathy may find Dave less than cooperative. He forgets to pick up the extra groceries as he was asked to do, and is not available to help clean the house in preparation. He may become drunk during the evening or be unfriendly to their guests. In the end, neither one of them enjoys the evening.

Variations of this theme can happen often in relationships that do not take account of the two different styles. What is needed here is a balance of planned and spontaneous events—an understanding, for instance, that some weekends are planned and some are left open. It is interesting that in some eastern cultures it is considered very rude to put someone on the spot with a direct question that requires an immediate answer. When that happens, it is considered quite acceptable, for example, to say yes to a dinner invitation and then not show up.

A more serious situation can develop when the perceptive partner makes a habit of going along with the judging partner's decisions, believing that it is better to give up his/her own needs than deal with the potential conflict. This situation develops especially with introverted perceptives who are also "feeling" types (see the next chapter). The difficulty here is that the judging type usually has no idea that his/her partner is doing this and believes that they have a perfect relationship with no disagreements. The perceptive type resents having constantly to comply, feeling that, in a good relationship, his/her partner would understand this difficulty with conflict and read his/her mind. Eventually perceptive types in this situation become so distant that they decide to leave. This comes as a shock to their judging partners, who believed they were so well suited to each other. Or, the situation may come to a head when the perceptive ones, after many years, decide to stand firm on a certain issue and are not taken seriously; they believed, erroneously, that their mates knew they were giving up their interests all those years.

In this case, if you are a perceptive type, you need to read carefully the later chapter on dealing with conflict and state your needs before it's too late. Your judging partner will not know that you have different needs unless you say so. Tell him/her that you find disagreements difficult and check to ensure that your disagreement is not causing hurt or damaging your relationship. In time, as you become reassured by your partner, you will become more confident in addressing differences between you.

PLANNING SOCIAL EVENTS

Judging types and perceptive types prepare for social events in different ways. When Cathy is preparing for her dinner party to be held on Saturday, she will plan it well ahead of time. By Monday she will have a clear idea of what she will be cooking and may even have prepared some dishes for the freezer. Most of the groceries will have been bought already. She may clean the house several days before and complain when her family continues to mess it up. On the other hand, Dave goes about things in a very different way. He will often shop for groceries on the day of the dinner party and decide what they will eat while in the grocery store. If he remembers, he will organize the house cleanup the night before; otherwise, it will be done in a frenzy during cooking. Both Dave and Cathy are capable, each in their own way, of having a decent meal prepared and presented on time in a clean and tidy household—although Dave may have the guests help set the table!

The difficulty here is the lack of understanding of each other's style. Dave becomes irritated with Cathy's need to plan so early, especially if she requires his help. He cannot understand why the house has to be cleaned and tidied so early when it will only get messy again. He becomes annoyed when Cathy complains all week about every cup or newspaper not put away. He does not see why he has to get these grocery items right now when there are still several days left before Saturday. Cathy, on the other hand, becomes increasingly anxious all week as she watches Dave carrying on with his life as usual. How can he possibly get everything done on time if he doesn't prepare in advance? She may continually ask him what they will be eating and when he will be starting preparations. Dave may perceive Cathy's anxiety as lack of trust that he can do a good job, and this may undermine his confidence. All the above will cause mounting tension between them as the week progresses.

The thing to remember here is that both of them are capable of doing a good job *if they are left to do it the way they know best.* Perceptive types will run into last-minute problems, but they are flexible and can adapt their plans to take account of them. If you're not the one responsible for organizing an event, it generally runs more smoothly if you give the organizer the support to do it his/her own way—however crazy you think the method of organization is. This may cause you inconvenience, but in the end you have the advantage of much less tension in the household. A bonus advantage of this strategy is that each of you can watch the other's style and learn from it. Eventually you may find a middle ground that embodies the strengths of both approaches.

TO KEEP OR THROW AWAY?

What merits keeping and what should be thrown away can cause difficulty between judging types and perceptive types. Cathy, as a judging personality, likes order and tidiness. When a magazine has been read, it seems sensible to throw it away; or, if there is an interesting article, it can first be cut out and filed. Dave, however, does not like to throw anything away. How will he know if at some future date he might need to reread an article that does not seem significant right now? Similarly, that shirt may come back into fashion, that chair just needs the leg mended, that sofa might be useful if they ever built an extension, those leftover vegetables will make a good soup at the weekend, those pieces of wood are bound to be useful for something, sometime. . . .

As you can see, large areas of space can be taken up with Dave's store of potentially useful items. This drives Cathy crazy. Occasionally she might try to remove something, thinking it will never be missed. To Cathy's astonishment, Dave knows exactly what he has and will certainly notice when it's gone. Many couples fight each other on this one in silence, the judging type removing things and the perceptive type collecting even more. This difference between them needs to be discussed and negotiated. The house has only so much space, but on the other hand certain stored items can often be useful. Find a compromise that works for both of you.

ORGANIZED VERSUS DISORGANIZED

Judging types feel more comfortable in an environment where things are put away in an organized manner. Perceptive types are much happier and, believe it or not, can find things much easier, when they are in a disorganized jumble. Dave, as the perceptive type, will not be happy when Cathy tidies his papers or organizes his desk. He will complain that he can no longer find anything. Cathy will be upset when Dave riffles through her papers looking for something and then leaves them in disarray. This is not too much of a problem when it relates to their individual space. However, shared space can be a big problem. When you and your partner are irritated by each other's style it is important to remember that each of you operates best in your chosen style. It is not that the perceptive type is a lazy, scattered, cluttered, creator of chaos and that the judging type is an uptight, controlling, sterile environment-creating neat freak. When you make these judgments you are not respecting the other's style and that makes it easier to be angry and irritated. When you understand that each operates more comfortably in his/her own chosen environment, then it is easier to be tolerant and find an operable solution.

PUNCTUALITY

Judging types and perceptive types have very different ideas about time commitments. When Cathy says she wants to meet at eight o'clock, she means eight o'clock, not anytime between eight and eight-thirty. When Dave says he wants to meet at eight o'clock, he really means sometime around eight o'clock. If you are a judging/perceptive couple, you may want to be clear what your time expectations are; otherwise you may end up with a spoilt evening. Similarly, when Dave goes out he may say he'll only be an hour. When Dave says this it does not mean he will be back in an hour. It means that he might only be an hour or he might be back in three, depending on what comes up. When Cathy says she will be an hour, she will be an hour. If she thinks she might be three hours, she will say so. Most judging types living with perceptive types have learned to add an hour or two to their partners' time estimates.

IN SUMMARY

So let's review how judging types and perceptive types differ:

- Judging and perceptive types may mishear each other on decisions: judges hear things as decided when they are not, and perceptives hear things as not yet decided when they are.
- Judging types are stressed when a decision is left "on hold." Perceptive types are stressed when they have to commit to a decision too early.
- Judging types may make decisions before they have all the facts. Perceptives will delay a decision even when they have gathered all the facts.
- Perceptive types prefer to decide their holiday plans at the last minute. Judging types like to plan well ahead of time.
- Perceptive types enjoy holidays that are unstructured with lots of room for variety. Judging types like a holiday that they can plan in detail so they can be sure to make the best use of their time.
- Judging types need closure on a decision or plan and may therefore argue their points quite forcefully. The perceptive types' wish to avoid conflict at all costs may lead them to avoid these discussions and appear passive-aggressive.
- When judging types argue their case strongly, perceptive types, in order to avoid conflict, may appear to agree even when they don't. This can have serious repercussions for the long-term relationship.
- Judging types are most comfortable planning for social events well in advance. Perceptives are most comfortable planning and doing at the same time—i.e., the last minute!
- Perceptive types like to save items and are very uncomfortable throwing things away. Judging types like to clear out unwanted or unneeded items.
- Judging types like to live in an orderly environment where everything has its place and should be put back there.

Perceptive types enjoy having all their things within reach and like to keep them there.

- Perceptive types have a flexible attitude toward time commitments. Judging types are committed to their time arrangements and expect that same commitment from others.

You will notice that, in most cases with this difference in style, compromise is the key. These styles work against each other in so many ways that finding a middle ground is the only way to accommodate both of them. It is reassuring to know that these particular style differences are less set than the others and may become less extreme as people age.

Chapter 3

Am I Emotional or Logical?

An individual's decision-making is influenced strongly by the way he/she comes to conclusions. One way of reaching a conclusion is by using a logical process: what seems fair and right in this situation? Another way is by using an emotional process: what would be the most comfortable decision based on personal values? People with these different approaches to decision-making, when in a relationship together, have difficulty understanding the validity of the other's rationale for decision-making. The former type of decision-maker is known as a **thinking type,** while the latter is known as a **feeling type**.

Thinking types:

- value a reasonable and fair decision
- are distressed by unfair decisions
- are task-focused in their communication
- can be quite critical of themselves and others
- enjoy conversation that is to the point
- have little patience with an emotional solution to a problem

- can be quite distressed by any show of emotion in their partners
- often see displays of emotion as a weakness and therefore keep their feelings to themselves
- enjoy appreciation of their competence

If most of the above applies to you then you are probably a thinking type (T).

Feeling types:

- value a solution that takes the impact on people and themselves into account
- are more likely to be forgiving of others
- value themselves for their warm and supportive nature
- enjoy prolonged conversations—the connection is more important than the information that is shared
- like to express their feelings (although this is more difficult for introverted feeling types)
- feel close to people that express their feelings
- get such satisfaction out of pleasing others that they will often sacrifice their own needs in order to do so
- may have little tolerance for a rational solution to a relationship problem
- like to be appreciated for just being there

If most of the above applies to you, then you are probably a feeling type (F).

These two personality traits are the only ones that have a male/female bias. Men are more likely to be thinking types and women are more likely to be feeling types; but it is not as large a difference as cultural stereotypes might suggest. With a male-dominant culture and a growing belief over the past two hundred and fifty years that using logical reasoning is the only valid way to come to a decision, the thinking style has become our culture's preference. However, relationships are much better defined in the words of feelings and emotions. No one ever wrote a task-focused love letter!

This denial of the validity of the emotional style has hindered the development of many satisfying relationships. Both styles need to be honoured, and in both individuals. It is not just a matter of creating a respectful balance of personality in the relationship, but also of developing balance in each partner. Feeling types need to be able to express their thoughts, opinions and needs clearly and concisely; and thinking types need to be able to express their feelings. When couples are unable to do this, they become distant and lose touch with the qualities that brought them together. This will also be true when both individuals are thinking types, or both are feeling types.

Now let's look at some of the difficulties feeling and thinking types experience. For illustration, I will introduce three more couples. The first couple is Ed and Fran. Ed is a thinker and Fran a feeling type. The second couple, Greg and Helen, are counter to the stereotype: Greg is a feeling type and Helen is a thinker. The third couple, Iris and John, are both thinkers.

APPRECIATION

Feeling and thinking types give and enjoy appreciation in different ways. Ed and Helen, the thinking types, like to be appreciated for what they achieve and the tasks they perform. They are both more likely to express their affection by doing something for their partners than by telling them that they love them. They show appreciation for things done for them when they remember—but often forget to do so. Ed and Helen can survive well without encouragement, and may assume the same to be true of their partners. A typical thinking type once told me, "I said I loved her when I married her; why do I need to say it again? Nothing's changed."

Fran and Greg, however, like to be appreciated for just being there. They like to hear that they look nice and that they are appreciated as companions. They continually do small things for their partners but don't consider them to be acts of love. They expect the same treatment from their partners. Fran and Greg enjoy continual encouragement and the affirmation of their importance to their partners. They can feel literally starved without it.

As you can see, feeling and thinking types may well miss reaching each other when trying to show appreciation. Each will believe they are being appreciative of their partners, but are showing it in the way that works for them. Consequently, their efforts are likely to be in vain. If your relationship is a mix of feeling and thinking then give appreciation *in a way that works for your partner* as well as the way that works for you. This will allow you to give your partner what he/she wants as well as modelling what you want. If you are both the same type, it is still important to validate both styles. After all, thinking people can be very sensitive, and feeling people can be logical. Mood swings and stress can temporarily change our preferred style, so it is always preferable to have a mix of both.

AFFECTION

Generally speaking, feeling types are much more comfortable with giving and receiving affection. Fran and Greg, the feeling types, enjoy hugging and sitting close together with their partners. They enjoy holding hands when out walking with their partners and appreciate a lot of physical contact.

Ed and Helen, the thinking types, are uncomfortable with too much physical contact. Remember that they see shows of emotion as weakness, and even when their brains know this is no longer true, their guts refuse to agree. The fact that they find demonstrations of affection difficult says nothing about the depth of their feeling, although their feeling partners often believe that it does. They may not be comfortable expressing their feelings, but that does not mean they don't have any.

Consequently, relationships are more of a challenge to thinking types; the expression of feeling and caring is what keeps relationships alive and prevents them from becoming simple business arrangements. Boys were raised not to show their feelings, as doing so would likely make them targets for bullies. Boys were also rewarded for keeping their cool when under attack. The traditional upbringing of boys has made it doubly hard for male thinkers in relationships. Girls were given more hugs and their expressions of emotion were far more tolerated. This gives women, even thinking women, an advantage.

Development of the opposite trait can be a highly positive experience for all individuals in couples. For feeling types, to respect the independence of their thinking partners and develop some of that independence in themselves can be a very liberating process. For thinking types, allowing themselves to respect and express their feelings will help them feel more in touch with themselves. Learning from each other can enrich the lives of both partners.

DEALING WITH CONFLICT

Thinking and feeling types come to decisions using different processes, which interfere considerably with successful conflict resolution. The most forceful of decision-makers is the thinker who is also an extroverted judging type. The individual who has the most difficulty coming to decisions and communicating them is the feeling type who is also introverted and perceptive. Ed is the former type and Fran is the latter.

When Ed, the extroverted, thinking judging type (ETJ) makes decisions, he communicates with confidence (extrovert) using logical reasoning (thinking), and is impatient to put his decision into action (judging). Fran, the introverted, feeling perceiver (IFP), finds it very difficult under pressure to organize her thoughts into a decision (perceptive), and even more difficult to communicate the result under pressure (introvert). This effort is usually too much for her and she agrees with Ed to please him (feeling) and keep the peace (perceptive). Ed believes that Fran agrees with him, not understanding that she is intimidated by his forcefulness and disabled by his impatience for a quick solution.

This pattern of behaviour worked for many years until their youngest child, Jenny, started school. Fran had been planning that, as soon as this happened, she would go back to her job as a teacher. She had not shared this plan with Ed, thinking that it was obvious. She had given up teaching to be with the kids while they were little and planned to go back when the last one started school. When she announced to Ed that she was going back to work, he was shocked. He had just been promoted and his workload had doubled. He could not see how their family could survive with them both working full time. They had survived so far on one salary. Surely they could wait a few more years until Ed's job was more settled. Fran surprised Ed by not backing down. She was determined to return to work and was unaffected by his arguments.

The impasse created anger on both sides and eventually distance. Ed was angry that Fran was not willing to compromise. He felt that she had ceased to care about him and had suddenly become a selfish stranger. Fran was angry that Ed would not support her in her decision when, during all the previous years of their marriage, she had ignored her own wishes in order to please him. She felt that he must not care about her at all if he could not support her this one time, and that he must, at heart, be a totally selfish person. These beliefs led them to the conviction that there was nothing left of their marriage, and they began to consider separating.

The above example may seem extreme, but I have seen variations of it happen over and over again. If you recognize this pattern in your own relationship, then you need to act immediately. Often it is already too late when these couples come in for counseling; the pattern of dominance and self-sacrifice has been going on for too long. For this story to have a positive ending, Fran needs to learn to share her thoughts and assert her beliefs so that, even if she eventually gives in, Ed will be aware that she has done so. Fran will need to ask for more time and resist the pressure to go along with instant decisions. She will have to believe that Ed cares about her and will respect her opinions if she can share them. She may need to take a course on assertiveness or get some counseling to help her change her response to Ed. These steps will be well worth it, as a rewarding relationship is not possible when one of the pair is unable to share wishes and opinions. Ed will also need to respect Fran's need for time to consider decisions, and to encourage and invite her to share what she believes.

Remember: we cannot expect our partners to know what we are thinking unless we tell them; and if you are in a relationship with an introvert, your partner won't share what he or she thinks unless invited to do so.

Another combination that may have difficulty handling conflict are the thinking judging (TJ) and the feeling judging types (FJ), especially when they are both introverted. Helen is the former and Greg is the latter.

When Helen makes a decision, she thinks about it carefully (introverted) using a logical thinking process (thinking) and comes to her best decision before sharing it (judging). When Greg makes a decision, he thinks about it carefully (introverted) using a value-based decision process (feeling) and comes to his best decision. When both Helen and Greg share what they have decided, they are both committed to their decisions. Neither wants to give way to the other, especially when the other's thought processes are both unknown and suspect. Helen and Greg need to develop their **extroversion** in order to share and promote understanding of their thinking or feeling process, and their **perception** in order to compromise.

EMOTIONAL SUPPORT

Feeling types use the phrase "emotional support" as if its meaning were quite obvious. Thinking types are often confused when their feeling partners ask for emotional support. They may feel unsure of what is expected of them. They do not understand that emotional support means hugging, listening (even when bored), a smile of encouragement, holding hands, or an arm around the shoulder. Generally when thinking and feeling types live together, the thinking types learn to understand the value of emotional support and will learn from their feeling partners how to be emotionally supportive.

EMOTIONAL SUPPORT WHEN TWO THINKING TYPES ARE INVOLVED

However, when both partners are thinking types, there is no feeling type to model emotional support. Strong thinkers can become very emotional when under stress and expect their confused partners to support them emotionally—something they have not expected before. Iris and John are both thinkers. They are effective as a team and are able to carry out the tasks associated with running a family and managing a relationship very well. However, when John loses his job, he becomes distressed and wants comfort from Iris. He feels abandoned by her when left to handle his distress alone. Although John believes he should be able to cope, he would nevertheless like Iris to comfort him. Although he does not have the words to express the deep feelings he is experiencing, he still resents the fact that Iris is not there for him. John suddenly expects to be coddled like a child and feels that Iris should stay home and look after his dependency needs rather than live her usual independent life. Iris wonders, "Who is this stranger?"

For Iris and John, this situation may herald a positive turning point. They may both begin to value a more emotional context to their relationship, and their dynamic may change from independent to interdependent. If this shift does not happen, the relationship generally becomes more distant and, over time, deteriorates.

CAREER CHOICES

Helen, the thinker, and Greg, the feeling type, may have very different career aspirations that may not fulfil the expectations of the culture in which they live. Helen, the more extroverted of the two, is ambitious and is doing very well in her career as an accountant. She earns more than Greg and works longer hours. Greg enjoys his work as a massage therapist, and has no ambitions to work more than his five shortened days each week. It gives him time with the kids after school and to write his column for the local paper. Both enjoy the career choices they have made, and the balance of intensity works well while they are raising a family.

Helen and Greg get into difficulties when their feelings about the relationship become tainted by cultural expectations. Helen begins to resent Greg's time with the kids and his more relaxed lifestyle. Although she enjoys Greg's relaxed nature and feels glad that he is there to spend time with the kids after school, there is a nagging suspicion that there must be something wrong with him. Men are supposed to work hard, be ambitious and earn more money. Greg begins to resent Helen's long hours and her expectation that he cook meals and do the grocery shopping.

Although Greg admires Helen's ambition and career success, there is a nagging suspicion that there must be something wrong with her. Women are supposed to look after domestic issues and defer to their husbands. Both feel inadequate and begin to resent each other, even though their relationship has up to now been working very successfully.

If you are a couple who make career or lifestyle choices that do not fit conventional expectations, then it is important for you to value what works well in the decisions you have made. You will need to recognize that your career decisions work well for you even if they do not meet societal expectations. Relationships between ambitious, task-focused men and easygoing, people-focused women have been considered acceptable for generations. There is no reason why the same qualities shouldn't be just as successful when the genders are reversed.

Ed, the thinking type, and Fran, the feeling type, may also get into difficulties. When they were first together, Ed and Fran both worked in jobs that did not pay that well and were not that satisfying. Before they had children, they made a decision that they would work hard, pay off their debts, and buy a small house. If things went as planned and they were able to save, they would find a way of life that was more rewarding. In the meantime, they would make the most of their leisure time, working out together and going to the theatre.

Things changed when the kids arrived. Fran became absorbed in their baby son and was nervous about leaving him with a babysitter. She was no longer interested in the leisure activities they had previously shared, and was too exhausted after the constant childcare to stay awake in the evening. Ed, who was still in his unsatisfying job, felt abandoned. He wanted to be involved with the baby but there seemed no space for him. He no longer had the leisure activities with his wife to look forward to. He felt unloved and began to spend evenings at work, hoping to develop a more satisfying work environment. Fran, exhausted, felt disappointed that Ed took no initiative in parenting and resented his absence in the evening. She did not want to make matters worse by confronting him with the issue.

When it came time for her to return to work, Fran realized she could never feel comfortable leaving her baby in daycare. She told Ed that she would prefer to stay home and raise their son and the second child they were planning to have in another year or two. Ed, who was beginning to enjoy his work more, agreed, but felt sad that they no longer went out together. He compensated for his disappointment by working harder and harder, with the rationale that there was only one salary now. Fran did not tell him about her increasing loneliness. She felt guilty that she was not making any money and felt she hadn't the right to complain.

For Ed and Fran's relationship to survive, they will need to find some time to devote to it and to themselves. Often just two or three hours a week without children present will be enough. Fran may need to cultivate a trusted babysitter and carry a cell phone so that she knows she can be contacted in case of emergency. Relationships will not survive the child-rearing stage if there is no connection between partners, now that the extended family (parents, parents-in-law, aunts) is no longer nearby or available for support.

SOCIABILITY

We know that introverts and extroverts differ in how much socializing they like to do. Feeling and thinking also affects how much and what kind of social interaction we enjoy. Feeling types like Fran and Greg enjoy interacting with people at any time just to connect with them. The subject or the point of the discussion is not important; if there is connection the interaction is worthwhile.

Thinking types like Ed and Helen enjoy interacting when there is a purpose. They have little patience with small talk and don't understand why their partners bother them with unfocused chitchat. Their obvious boredom may hurt their partners' feelings and may be interpreted as lack of love.

If you are a feeling type in a relationship with a thinking type and find it difficult to have satisfying verbal interactions, you may find it easier if you are careful to build communication around common projects such as parenting and gardening plans. If all you talk about is your relationship and your feelings, you may find that your thinking partner will tune you out.

If you are a thinking type in a relationship with a feeling type, then you will need to listen actively (see Chapter 5) to your partner's emotional outbursts without rolling your eyeballs (!) and be willing occasionally to spend time on purposeless chatter.

IN SUMMARY

Now let's review how thinking and feeling types differ:

- Thinking types like to be appreciated for what they achieve. Feeling types like to be appreciated for just being there.
- Feeling types verbally express appreciation. Thinking types express their appreciation by doing something nice for their partner. Apologies are dealt with in a similar way.
- Feeling types are comfortable expressing affection verbally and non-verbally. Thinking types are not naturally comfortable in the emotional world.
- Thinking types are direct, sometimes even blunt, in order to make a point. Feeling types are indirect, sometimes to the extreme of obscurity.
- Thinking types come from a rational viewpoint. Feeling types come from an emotional viewpoint.
- Feeling types may withdraw in the face of conflict. Thinking types may not realize when this has happened.
- Feeling types enjoy giving and receiving emotional support. Thinking types may need to learn how to give and receive this support.
- The male stereotype is a thinker; the female stereotype is a feeling type. When the types are reversed in a relationship, expectations may be confused.
- Feeling types put family time first and may give up time for themselves and their relationships when they have children. Thinking types are more likely to wish to continue their independent lifestyles and may feel

abandoned when their partners become absorbed in family issues.

- Thinking types like communication to be task-focused. Feeling types like to talk about anything at all—there just needs to be a verbal connection.

The above is a very general list of differences. Many or all of them may not apply if the couple has already worked hard at respecting their needs.

Chapter 4

Am I Practical or Creative?

The final two personality traits described by Jung are related to how we see the world. We can see things as they are and pay attention to the here and now, or we can perceive the world in terms of how it might be and pay attention to what happens next. The former the **sensing type** and the latter the **intuitive type.**

Sensing types:

- pay attention to the concrete, i.e., what they can perceive by seeing, hearing, touching, smelling and tasting
- live in and enjoy the present, without much concern about what will happen next
- may feel stuck when things go badly, unable to focus on a better future
- notice the details in the environment around them
- don't worry too much about the future except when stressed
- enjoy facts and clear data

- are uncomfortable with uncertainty and change
- value their practicality and good sense
- read the instructions
- can back up their opinions with evidence

If most of the above applies to you then you are probably a sensing type (S).

Intuitive types:

- often ignore what they perceive with their senses in favour of a gut feeling
- live in the future, often not noticing what is happening in the present
- may not address a difficult situation, assuming it will improve later
- may not notice the details and the environment around them
- see the forest rather than the trees
- enjoy looking for patterns and meaning in what they see
- enjoy ideas and dreams for the future
- enjoy uncertainty and change
- value their creativity (in problem solving and/or the arts) and good ideas
- may not read the instructions or follow the directions
- may have strong opinions with little evidence to support them

If most of the above applies to you then you are probably an intuitive type (N).

Of all personality differences, this one seems to cause the fewest problems related to communication in relationships. Couples seem to understand and appreciate the balance this difference can give to their partnership. In these examples, Karen is intuitive and Leo is the sensing type.

CREATIVE VERSUS PRACTICAL

Intuitive types enjoy the world of dreams and fantasy. They like to speculate in areas that are completely unknown and to share these thoughts with their partners. Sensing types cannot see the point in these dreams and speculations, and often "burst the bubble" with the facts. The intuitive type, who may as a result feel crushed and demeaned, rarely appreciates this realism.

Karen, the intuitive type, likes to brainstorm out loud. When she and Leo are planning a decorating project, she throws out a large number of ideas, only a few of which are practical. The excess of ideas overwhelms Leo, the sensing type. He dismisses most of them immediately, on the grounds of impracticality. Karen feels crushed and loses interest in the whole project.

If this happens in your relationship, remember that the intuitive partner's ideas may have merit when tempered with the sensing partner's practical outlook. Each partner needs to listen to the other so that the partnership gets the benefit of both approaches. The combination of sensing and intuition can produce novelty that works.

CARRYING OUT TASKS

Intuitive types who are also perceptive (the researchers) have many ideas but are not always interested in carrying them out. Sensing types who are also judging (the decision-makers) may enjoy putting plans into action. This creates a balance that works well in many relationships. However, for intuitives with the judging/perceptive styles reversed, there may be difficulties.

Karen is an intuitive judging type (NJ). She has an idea and she wants to see it put into action now. In order to carry out this idea, she requires Leo's expertise in practical matters. Leo is a sensing perceptive type (SP). When confronted with Karen's idea, he wants to research its practicality and be sure it will work before starting. Once the project is underway, he may get bored with it before it's finished. He may also resist Karen's idea because, having an independent nature, he would prefer to find his own way to do it. Karen becomes frustrated and angry when her idea is left to collect dust.

If you relate to Karen in this story, you have two options. You can learn the skills that you need in order to carry out your idea yourself. When you do this you will stop feeling so powerless. The usual difficulty with this route is that you may be moving into your partner's area of expertise, and either you may be afraid to do so, or your partner may be threatened by this invasion into his/her territory. If this is the case then you will require all your newly acquired communication skills to resolve the issue!

Karen: We agreed last year to paint the living room. You said you'd do it and bought the paint but have put off doing it. I'd really like to get it done before the winter, so I've decided to get it done this weekend.

Leo: I said I'd do it. I'll get it done in the fall, when the weather isn't so good.

Karen: No. You said that last year but when the fall came you were too busy with work. I'm the one who really wants it done, so I'd really like to do it.

Leo: Fine. But don't expect any help from me. I'm busy this weekend.

Karen: That's okay.

If you go this route, you might be surprised to find that when the time comes to do the task, you will get help after all.

The second option is to accept that you don't want to do the task yourself and therefore you cannot expect to have it done in your timeframe. You can state assertively how you feel about the delay:

Karen: When you agree to paint the living room but keep putting it off, I feel really frustrated. I know you want to do it yourself and I don't think I'd do such a good job. I'd really appreciate you doing it within the next month. Is there anything I could do that would help free up some time for you to paint?

Leo: I'll get it done soon.

And then later:

Karen: A month ago, you said you would get the living room painted soon and you've not started yet. I don't understand the delay and I'm beginning to feel that my wishes aren't important to you. I'd still like to get it done. What's going on?

Leo: I don't know. There's never enough time to do everything. I'll try to get it done next weekend.

And then later:

Karen: I realize that you don't have time to paint the living room so I've been saving up for the last couple of months to get a decorator. He's coming next weekend.

If you relate to Leo in the story it would be useful for you to consider what your delay achieves. Do you delay because you don't want to do the task but feel you should? If this is the case you may want to examine where this "should" is coming from and whether it really needs to rule your life and cause difficulties in your relationship. Often these "shoulds" come from outdated values, such as, "Men should do all the practical fixing in the house," or "Women should carry out all decisions related to children." They may also come from values in your family when you were a child, such as, "Women take care of finances," or "Men always book airline tickets." If this is so, you may find it useful to have a discussion with your partner to figure out which values and role stereotypes work for your relationship and which don't.

If you are being resistant because you don't like to be told what to do, then it's important to recognize that you are no longer a child. As an adult you choose to behave in the way that you do. When you do something for your partner, you choose to do it to please him/her or to help the relationship run smoothly. If you can keep this in mind it will help you feel in control of your decisions. (Intuitive-perceptive types also often take this rebellious stand against their partners.)

If you are a strong sensing-perceptive type who lives in the present and procrastinates on chores, you may want to develop your intuitive-judging side or your time management skills. Such types are often burdened by perpetual guilt and feel quite relieved not to have to deal with perpetually undone tasks and the resulting conflict.

TIDINESS

One difficulty that this difference in types creates is in the realm of lifestyle rather than communication. Sensing types like to live in an ordered household, and they notice when items are out of place. Intuitive types can live in chaos and don't notice when things are out of place, even when they are placed right in front of them. Leo, a typical sensing type, tidies up by placing items on the stairs for Karen to put away. Karen, a typical intuitive type, goes up and down the stairs numerous times without noticing them at all. She does not, therefore, put them away. Leo feels she is deliberately ignoring his non-verbal message, and he becomes angry.

If Leo wants Karen to put her things away, he will need to ask her to do so. Putting out-of-place items in her path is not effective; she will not notice them.

Related to this lack of attention to detail, intuitive types often do not notice when their partners have changed something in their appearance or in the décor of the house. For example, the intuitive type may not notice a new haircut or decorating job.

Karen, as mentioned before, is an intuitive-judging type. She may not notice her own mess but will be intolerant when Leo who, being perceptive, will often leave things out that are connected to his unfinished projects. Being of decisive nature, she takes charge by tidying his things away for him, a solution that upsets both of them: Karen resents having to clear up after Leo, and he resents having his things interfered with. In this case they will have to decide whether to develop more tolerance of each other's mess, or to become tidier.

RELATIONSHIP ANALYSIS

Intuitive types enjoy analyzing the relationship and figuring out why their partners act the way they do. This constant analysis can be very irritating to their sensing partners, who see no merit in explaining behaviour. "I am the way I am and that's all there is to it" is a typical sensing statement. Remember that sensing types live in the present and have little interest in analyzing the past. If you are an intuitive type and enjoy relationship analysis, you may want to reserve this pastime for when you are with like-minded friends!

However, when the relationship is in difficulty, the problem-solving skills of the intuitive type can be useful. In this case, a little analysis often may be worthwhile, especially when combined with the practical sensing approach. For example, it may be good for Leo to understand that he is afraid to let go of financial decision-making because his mother had spent unwisely throughout his childhood, leaving the family seriously in debt. However, the important issue here is not what happened in the past, but how to resolve financial decisions between Leo and Karen now. The combination of problem-solving skills and attention to detail gives much-needed balance.

GETTING TO THE POINT

Sensing and intuitive types get to the point in different ways. Leo, the sensing type, gets to the point step by step:

Leo: I went out for lunch today with Mike. We went to that restaurant on Main Street. You know—the one that just opened a couple of weeks ago. We had a great meal; you and I should go there sometime. Anyway, on the way back to work I passed a travel agent offering some great holiday deals. Mind you, the agent was on the phone and I had to wait ages before I could talk to her. I thought I was going to be really late for work. Anyway, she eventually got off the phone and I asked her about flights to Bermuda. They've got an amazing deal for one of those all-inclusive resorts. What do you think about going to Bermuda for Christmas?

While Leo is speaking, Karen may well switch off to avoid listening to all the detail; or she may interrupt and ask where he is headed.

If Karen wanted to share the same information, she would do it quite differently:

Karen: Guess what? It looks like we can afford to spend Christmas in Bermuda!

Karen starts with the point she wants to make. Leo, hearing this, panics. Since he has no information to work with, no facts to back up the decision, his initial response is very likely to be negative.

To be effective, you may have to adapt your style to your partner's in order for him/her to hear you. If you are intuitive and are communicating with a sensing type, you will be more effective if you state the facts before you come to the point. If you are sensing and are speaking to an intuitive type it will work better if you state the point first and then relay the details if necessary.

Somewhat related to the above is the difficulty the intuitive type may have with staying on topic. This is especially true for the intuitive-perceptive types, who often leave their sentences unfinished, either because they've changed their minds about what they have to say; or their minds, working faster than their speech, have already finished the sentence and they find it tedious to have to carry on speaking. Sometimes, for the same reason, they may jump from one topic to something that appears to their partners to be completely unrelated. They forgot to share the link. This perceived "scatterbrain" thinking is infuriating to their partners, who may give up trying to follow.

If you are the sensing partner, you can use your listening skills to get the missing information. You can also state assertively how you feel about your partner's mode of communication and what you would like changed:

Leo: When you jump from one topic to another that seems completely unrelated, I get confused about what you're trying to say. I wish you'd let me know how these topics are connected.

Or,

Leo: When you leave your sentences unfinished, I get infuriated. I wish you'd finish your sentences once you've started them.

If you are the intuitive partner, be understanding of your partner's frustration. Following your train of thought is difficult for him/her when you leave so much unsaid. You may think the omissions are self-explanatory, but they probably aren't.

It's important to recognize that individuals in relationships also leave their sentences unfinished when they are getting no attention from their partners. It's very hard to finish what you are saying when your partner is looking bored or at the newspaper or out the window.

IN SUMMARY

So now let's summarize how intuitive and sensing types differ:

- Sensing types notice untidiness in the house and are uncomfortable with it. Intuitive types do not notice mess and, while they may enjoy a tidy house, they would not make it a priority to clean up.
- Sensing types are likely to notice changes in their environment or in their partners' appearance and to remark on them. Intuitive types are less likely to notice these changes.
- Intuitive types like to dream and speculate. Sensing types like to keep their feet firmly on the ground. The sensing type's realism can dampen the intuitive type's enthusiasm.
- Intuitive types have the ideas but not always the practical skills to put them in motion. Sensing types have the practical skills to put ideas into action but may not have many ideas.
- Sensing types are skilled at dealing with the practicalities of getting the job done but may get stuck when a problem arises. Intuitive types are skilled in problem solving but may not be practical.
- Intuitive types like to analyze the relationship—what's happened in the past, and what may happen in the future. Sensing types like to live in the present and leave the past and future alone.
- Sensing types get to the point step by step. Intuitive types start with the point and give details only when necessary, if they remember them.
- Sensing types give all the facts to back up their statements. Intuitive types may confuse their partners by

leaving sentences unfinished, omitting details, or changing topics without explanation.

We have now finished the section on different personality types. In the next section of the book I will look at specific communication skills and how to use them constructively.

Chapter 5

Skills for Better Listening

I have found, in the classes I have taught, that the exercises I use are much easier for strangers than for couples. For example, one exercise looks at the ability to communicate clearly and listen to instructions. Two people sit back-to-back (so there are no non-verbal cues). The speaker has a diagram to convey, and the listener has to draw it. In the first part of the session, the listener is not allowed to speak but must just draw the diagram according to instructions (one-way communication). In the second part, a new diagram is displayed and the listener can ask questions and clarify (two-way communication).

The theory is that two-way communication is a far more efficient way of getting information across than one-way communication. I found that this was proven true for strangers. However when couples attempted this task, the reverse was often true. As soon as they were both involved in the verbal interaction, the whole process seemed to break down. On occasion, couples were actually unable to complete this simple exercise. What happened here? The task was the same for each pair. It seems that for couples in a relationship, information is taken in completely differently than for people who are not intimately involved. Let's look at why this might be.

ACTIVE VERSUS PASSIVE LISTENING

Unless told otherwise, most people believe that to listen requires that you remain quiet while the other person speaks. When you've heard what they have to say, you respond or withdraw depending on what has been said. The problem with this approach, called *passive listening,* is that the speaker has little idea that you are attending to them. **Showing attention is very important in relationships**. This involves the development of *active listening* skills.

For example, if you were to approach a stranger and ask for directions, and this stranger did not look at you while responding, you would probably still listen to the directions and find your way. However, if you made the same request of your partner and elicited this response, you might withdraw with hurt feelings, having retained little of the information received. Or you might respond angrily to this lack of attention and make a sarcastic comment like, "Sorry to distract you from the fascinating TV commercials"; or you might respond assertively with, "I wish you'd look at me while I'm talking to you." Whatever you did, however, you would probably not have accurately retained the information you were given. The body language you received interfered with the message.

In my communication classes, I would sometimes divide the class in half. One half would be "speakers," and were instructed to talk about what they had done the previous weekend. The other half were "listeners," and were instructed to be silent, look anywhere in the room but at the speaker, and to absolutely avoid all eye contact with him/her. After a very short time the noise level in the room would escalate considerably. Soon after that there was almost silence. A few individuals, who were used to talking to themselves, carried on. What happened here is repeated in a large number of couple relationships. One person speaks, perceives him/herself unheard, speaks louder or repetitively, and eventually gives up. The other, behind a newspaper or involved in some task, does not look at the speaker but listens passively, giving no indication that he or she has heard. Active listening skills are needed here.

WHAT ARE OUR GOALS AS LISTENERS?

What is the point of being an effective listener in an intimate relationship? Let's look at some possible goals that might encourage us to improve our listening skills:

- to build trust in the relationship
- to build safety so our partners will share with us
- to support our partners in problem solving
- to support our partners in emotional difficulty
- to encourage intimacy
- to be companionable
- to set the stage for ourselves to be heard

These are a few goals you may have and I am sure you can think of many others. When you are listening to your partner speak, you may need to remind yourself of your goal and avoid any behaviour that might detract from it.

TYPES OF BEHAVIOUR THAT SABOTAGE OUR LISTENING GOALS

There are many kinds of behaviour that can annihilate all the above goals very quickly. Examples are:

- interrupting
- changing the subject to our own concerns
- criticizing our partners
- denigrating the content
- insulting our partners
- picking up the newspaper to read
- switching on the TV
- analyzing our partners' feelings
- displaying inattentive body language
- using a hostile tone of voice

If you find that your partner gives up speaking to you suddenly or becomes hostile, then do a mental check to see whether you may have been doing any of the above. If you have, don't be surprised at the response you're getting. If you want the conversation to continue, you may need to apologize for inattentive or unsupportive behaviour and commit to a more supportive listening attitude. The skills mentioned below are important for showing both attention and support as a listener. It is important to remember that using these skills will feel very strange to start with. They may sound fake and "not you." They may not be you as an adult but they probably *were* you as a child. Children, when they are learning to speak and are not yet confident with their understanding of words, use these skills all the time. As you get to be a better listener, you will find that active listening will become more natural to you and you will find a way of wording your responses that feels more "you."

EXTROVERTS AND INTROVERTS AS LISTENERS

As mentioned in Chapter 1, extroverts and introverts listen in different ways. Annie, the extrovert, is much more active in her listening than Bob, who is an introvert. However, she will not always listen carefully to all the content before she gives her response. This type of listening would generally be no problem if she were married to an extrovert, as he would have no difficulty stating his thought again. But Bob is not comfortable having to repeat himself, and may prefer to give up. Annie will need to slow her response down when talking to him.

Bob, once Annie has his attention, has no difficulty with listening to the whole message and hearing it correctly. He is, however, not good at *active* listening. He often does not acknowledge Annie either verbally or non-verbally, so she thinks he does not listen to her. Bob needs to make a special effort to use the active listening skills mentioned below so that Annie knows he is listening.

NON-VERBAL LISTENING SKILLS

The most basic form of listening is non-verbal. Although we can actually deploy non-verbal skills without listening, it is very difficult to talk to people when they don't give these cues. We give the most important non-verbal message with our eyes. By looking at those who are speaking to us, we tell them that they have got our attention. If we actually turn around and face them and smile encouragement, we inform them that we have some time to give them. If we add encouraging noises, this is a bonus. We can even add neutral comments such as, "I see . . . " or, "That's interesting!" However, it is possible to do all this without listening to a word the other is saying. All we've shown so far is that we can give up some time to observe our partners speaking. Now, there are times when this type of listening is very useful. If your partner is venting angry feelings and just wants an audience, then you probably don't *want* to hear all the content. However, if that anger is directed at you, then this mode of listening is not useful for either of you.

Open body language is also a part of non-verbal listening skills. When you are open to hearing your partner, your body faces him or her and you may smile encouragement. Hostile body language such as glaring, fist clenching, or pointing will freeze your partner in his/her tracks. Tone of voice is part of body language, too. As you use the following more advanced listening skills, you will need to be sure that your body language and tone of voice match your supportive listening.

PARAPHRASING OR RESTATING

The next level of listening and probably the most important skill of all is when you paraphrase or restate what you have heard. Generally the only individuals who do this are therapists, small children, and individuals who have learned how to communicate effectively. This form of listening is a precious gift to give to your partner. It says, "I'm here, I have the time and I'm interested in what you're saying." When Annie comes home at the end of the day and says, "I've had a horrible day at work," there's a huge difference between the response, "Uh-huh" and the response, "Oh, you had a really bad day today?" The former simply tells Annie that she was heard speaking. The latter response is an invitation for Annie to continue and announces that Bob cares about her feelings.

Paraphrasing is useful in many other ways. Often statements we hear are unclear or ambiguous. Paraphrasing the message that we thought we heard can be very useful:

Annie: It's a real mess in here!

Bob: Are you saying that I should have cleared up before you came home?

Annie: Oh no, I just thought we should spend some time clearing up this evening.

Although "It's a mess in here" is only a statement, almost 100% of the couples I have seen have interpreted these simple words as a criticism. If it is seen as such, then any number of responses can result: "Well, clean it up yourself. Why should I do all the work around here?" or, "I'm sorry, I guess I'm useless at keeping the place tidy." Or no comment at all, but withdrawal accompanied by an angry or sad face. If the initial comment was not meant to be a criticism, then the original speaker can be baffled by this response and also may become angry or withdrawn.

What if, you might say, the comment was *meant* to be a criticism? If that is so, you will still do better by paraphrasing:

Bob: Supper's late again!

Annie: Are you saying that you wish that I'd managed to get supper done on time?

Bob: Yes, I'm in a rush on Tuesday nights and have been late for my hockey game for the last two weeks.

When you paraphrase, you encourage your partner to be more assertive. Next time, Bob may start the conversation with his second statement followed by a request for supper to be on time.

In another scenario, your partner might not admit to making the criticism. This is especially true of IFPs like Fran:

Fran: You're going out again.

Ed: Are you saying that I'm going out too much?

Fran: No, it's fine (said with a despondent look).

Ed: Great, I'll see you later then.

In this case, if Fran wants to get her message across, next time she will need to be more direct. When Ed gets home, Fran may well be angry and uncommunicative. How to deal with that will be covered in a later chapter.

We can never win by responding to statements as if they are criticisms without checking them out first to be certain of their meaning.

Paraphrasing is also useful for dealing with unfair angry statements. EFs and ETs, when under stress, will sometimes come out with strong emotional statements:

Annie: I hate you. You're never on time. I wish I'd never met you.

Bob: Are you saying that you hate me and wish you'd never met me because I'm late?

In this case, Bob confronts Annie with the injustice of her statement. Paraphrasing can also be helpful when your partner is muddled and unsure of what he/she wants to say. Often when you paraphrase back a muddled statement, your partner is able to restate more clearly what he/she originally wanted to say or even to figure out a more precise way of conveying the message. Perceptive types, especially if they are also intuitive, may well come across like John in the following exchange:

John: I'm thinking of going to see Jo this weekend, though I guess the basement needs finishing.

Iris: You're thinking of visiting Jo this weekend though the basement needs finishing?

John: Yeah, I'd like to visit Jo this weekend. Would you mind if we left the basement 'til next weekend?

By paraphrasing what she hears, Iris helps John organize his thoughts better.

REFLECTIVE LISTENING

Reflective listening is somewhat similar to paraphrasing but tends to show a deeper and more active commitment to the speaker. Here, you listen to the content, maybe paraphrasing so as to hear all that your partner needs to say. You then consider how your partner might be feeling, given all that was just said; and lastly you share how you think he/she might be feeling. Feeling types are often pretty good at reflective listening. Thinkers may need to use it more often:

Ed: You're telling me that your boss came into your office and shouted at you in front of Cathy and Debbie, criticizing that report you spent all weekend doing? (restating) You must have felt so embarrassed and really mad that he didn't recognize all your hard work. (Reflective response.)

Fran: Yeah, I just wanted to punch him in the face.

This kind of listening, sometimes also called *empathic* listening, is really rewarding for the speaker. In this case, it tells Fran that Ed is really hearing her. He has put himself in her shoes and thought about how he might feel if this had happened to him. The ability to put yourself in your partner's shoes occasionally is seen as one of the main components of a successful relationship. Unfortunately, few of those who are able to be empathic actually put this ability into practice with those closest to them.

Sometimes we may get the message wrong, but this doesn't matter. We are still showing that we are actively thinking about what we are hearing. The following might be a typical interaction between Karen and Leo:

Karen: You're saying that after all that planning, John's decided not to do that canoe trip with you next summer? You must be feeling quite disappointed. (Reflective response.)

Leo: No—I feel quite relieved, really. I was beginning to think we'd have a hard time getting along. He seems to always want things his way.

In this case, although Karen guessed wrongly about how Leo might be feeling, when she replied with her empathic response, he was able to share how he really felt about the trip—information she hadn't heard from him before.

CLARIFIYING OR QUESTIONING

Asking questions about what we hear is the piece of active listening that we often do quite well. Questions can be used to get more information:

Annie: I'm going out to the mall around eleven o'clock.

Bob: Does that mean that you won't be back for lunch?

Or they may be used to explore more sides of the problem at hand:

Bob: I can't decide whether to take that contracting job or not. (Having already explained all the issues.)

Annie: Are you most bothered about not having a secure salary or is it more to do with working with Ken again?

Although questions can be useful sometimes, what they may often do is put the speaker on the spot. Remember, introverts hate being put on the spot and may respond defensively like Bob in the following exchange:

Bob: I guess we haven't seen my mum this month.

Annie: Are you thinking of going to see her this weekend? (She has other plans.)

Bob: You never want to spend time with her.

When the subject is a touchy one between you, paraphrasing and reflective listening are much safer than questions. With a question, sometimes the tone of voice can give a cue as to whether you are being supportive or critical, as in Annie's question above.

I have found, while working with couples, that questions beginning with "why" are rarely effective. These questions seem to put partners on the spot, resulting in a defensive answer. If you have kids, you'll know how frustrating these questions are; and how as parents we will often answer, "just because," when we can't be bothered to think of justifications any longer.

When you want to ask a "why" question, see if you can rephrase it starting with "what" or "how." For example:

What were you thinking when you . . .?

Instead of,

Why did you . . .?

And

How did you get to be late?

Instead of,

Why are you late?

Yes, the meaning is the same. For some reason the results are better. Why? Questions tend to trigger the rebellious child in us!

SUMMARIZING

This active listening technique is useful when you have a whole lot of information coming at you and you need to be sure you've got it right. Introverts often find it a useful technique to ensure that they have retained all the information their extroverted partners have thrown at them all at once:

Bob: So you're saying that Mark has hockey on Monday night and you need the car, so we need to arrange a ride for him there, but you should be able to pick him up. On Thursday you've arranged a pickup for Alice's figure skating but you'll need me to drive her home because you're working late. Have I got that right?

This technique may also be useful when doing future planning or negotiating different decisions on how to spend money or holidays. Sometimes, even when people paraphrase information accurately they may still get it wrong. This can happen if a wrong assumption has distorted the understanding. ETs like Ed will often react this way, as they tend to come to conclusions quickly without hearing all the information. With luck this mistaken thinking will come out at the summarizing stage:

Ed: So you've decided not to take the two weeks off in May because your workload is going to be too heavy at that time. You'll probably take time off by yourself the last two weeks in June when work is usually calmer and your sister is going to be in town.

Fran: Yeah, but I never said I wanted to take time off by myself.

Ed: Well, I'm on a course the last two weeks of June.

Fran: Oh, I forgot that. I guess we'll have to think again.

As you can see from the above interaction, summarizing can pick up mistaken assumptions before any damage is done.

LISTENING RATHER THAN PROBLEM-SOLVING

It is often tempting to support our partners by solving problems for them. We can feel helpful when we do this, and won't feel so powerless as we watch them struggle through an issue. However, our partners very rarely appreciate this support. From their point of view we are seen as taking over their problems, interfering, or trying to control their lives. Individuals who are both thinking and judging, like Bob and Ed, are particularly likely to do this. Unless you have been specifically asked for your input, it is usually safer simply to listen empathetically and let him/her sort it out alone. If you have an aching desire to say something useful, ask permission first. If it is denied, let it go:

Fran: I can't decide whether to go to Debbie's housewarming.

Ed: Are you asking me what I think about it?

Fran: No, I've just got to figure out whether it's important enough for me to juggle everything else around it.

Ed: Okay.

If you are invited to give an opinion or want to give one anyway, avoid starting your sentence with, "You should." However these two words are said, they are almost always seen as belittling and perceived as a statement of inadequacy. Many people habitually use "should" statements and don't mean to be demeaning. It doesn't matter what you *mean* to convey if the message is perceived as something different and seen as unsupportive. This is one of the situations where one word or the lack of it can change the whole feeling of the message. **The word "should" is better left out of *all* couples' communication.**

Active listening skills are probably the most important ingredient of a successful relationship. While other skills and pieces of knowledge are useful, we can survive the lack of a good number of them if we listen in an active, supportive way. In the next chapter we will look at rules for communicating directly in a way that conveys a sense of caring and respect for our partners.

Chapter 6

How to be Better Understood

Communicating effectively as a speaker in a couple relationship can be very difficult. Generally, effective communication requires first of all that we state clearly and concisely what we want, and that we have credibility as speakers. This sounds easy, but somehow it isn't. In a work environment, if we need help to complete a particular project, we go to the appropriate person and request help. At home, making even a simple request for help can be hard. There are many reasons for this. Most of them are based on the unreal expectations we have, due to outdated beliefs and values.

SELF-DEFEATING BELIEFS

Self-defeating beliefs interfere seriously with our ability to communicate competently. Examples of such beliefs might be:

- My partner should look after my needs.
- My partner should love me unconditionally at all times.
- My partner should know what I want without my having to ask.

- If I feel angry/irritated/annoyed with my partner, there is something wrong with our relationship.
- If my partner ever feels angry/irritated/annoyed with me then there is something wrong with our relationship.
- If my partner doesn't agree with me then it means he or she doesn't respect me.
- Good relationships don't have disagreements.
- Good relationships are maintained with no effort.
- If we have problems, we can't be suited to each other.
- If my partner doesn't listen to me, then it means he or she doesn't love me.
- If my partner doesn't want to make love, then it means he or she doesn't love me.

You can probably think of others on your own.

When you read all these statements, how many of them do you believe? How often does this kind of thinking interfere with how you communicate with your partner, or block you altogether? It may even surprise you that these beliefs are unrealistic. If so, be aware that you will likely not be satisfied with your relationship and will always have a great deal of difficulty communicating with your partner, even when you do have the necessary skills. While we have these self-defeating beliefs, we find it difficult to be direct and may also feel resentful that we have to be direct before our message is heard. We just wish our partners could read our minds and respond in a helpful, supportive way. If this sounds like you, I suggest you read *Love is Never Enough* by Dr. Aaron Beck.

USEFUL REPLACEMENT STATEMENTS

Some useful self-statements we can make to replace the above self-defeating beliefs are suggested below:

- I am responsible for myself.
- I want to be treated with respect and will ensure that my partner understands that.

- I have the responsibility to express my feelings.
- I have the responsibility to share my expectations of my partner with him/her.
- I have the responsibility to state my wishes.
- I want to be listened to and will do what I can to ensure that.
- I can say no without feeling guilty.
- I can disagree if I do it respectfully.
- If we have problems, we can work through them together.
- When we disagree, we can learn from each other.

You can add more of your own. If we can replace irrational beliefs with this kind of thinking, we will have more confidence and be more in charge of our lives.

WHAT ARE OUR GOALS AS SPEAKERS?

What is the point of being an effective speaker in an intimate relationship? To be effective as a communicator, it is important to be aware of what we want to achieve. Often when we are annoyed with something a partner has said or done, we forget that our ultimate goal is to change that particular kind of behaviour. Instead, we want to make sure our partner suffers for acting that way. While this may be satisfying in the short term, it does nothing to improve the situation or the relationship.

Here are a few goals we may have when speaking that will ensure the interaction is constructive:

- to share our beliefs
- to share our feelings
- to help our partners know us better
- to treat our partners with respect
- to share information and ideas
- to encourage our partners to also share with us
- to discuss plans

- to point out behaviour we don't like
- to be companionable
- to maintain connection
- to pass time together

You can probably think of many more, and some may be more important than others. When you are speaking and things are not going as you might wish, you may need to remind yourself of your goal and ask yourself whether you are communicating in a way that will get you there.

BEHAVIOURS THAT SABOTAGE OUR GOALS AS SPEAKERS

There are many ways we can ensure that our communication will **not** be effective:

- hostile or defensive body language
- hostile or sarcastic tone of voice
- blaming
- accusing
- making faulty assumptions
- acting on irrational beliefs
- generalizing
- labelling

When your communication is not working, then somehow you are behaving in a manner that is sabotaging your ultimate goal. The following guidelines will help you to be aware of approaches that are more likely to lead the way to respectful and constructive interactions.

SO HOW CAN WE BE DIRECT?

To convey our needs and feelings clearly, we need to think before we speak. In couples' communication, the first thoughtless words that come out of our mouths may head us onto a disaster course. So now let's look at how to avoid this.

OWN YOUR MESSAGE

The first and most important rule of clear communication is to openly *own* your message by using first person singular pronouns (I, my): "I feel sad about . . . " or "I'd like to . . . "

Personal ownership clearly demonstrates that you take responsibility for the ideas and feelings you are expressing, and is less threatening to the listener.

Using "I" is very difficult for many people, especially women raised in traditional households. If you are a woman, you may believe that saying "I want . . . " or "I feel . . . " sounds pushy and demanding—adjectives that do not jibe well with femininity. Most women were taught to equate assertive behaviour with aggression or masculinity. Many individuals, men and women, think that using "I" too much defines them as selfish and controlling, and they are fearful of appearing that way. It is certainly true that women in past generations were told they'd never get a husband if they were demanding, selfish or controlling. And men had great difficulty owning their feelings with "I" statements because men weren't supposed to be ruled by emotional responses; they believed this made them seem weak and vulnerable.

So what do we resort to when we can't speak for ourselves? The two words that are used most often to replace "I" are "you" and "it." We use these two words in phrases such as, "It makes me mad when you . . ." or "You make me mad when you . . ." instead of "I feel mad when you . . . "

"IT" STATEMENTS

Let's look at "it" first. This word begins a passive statement. Instead of owning our feeling, we give responsibility for the feeling to "it." When we are afraid of the response and use such statements, we feel powerless and often confuse our partners. Somehow, if we don't own the feeling, we won't get shouted at.

Unfortunately, most "it" statements are ignored altogether. They are so indirect that they make little impact on our audience. The most common response is an unspoken guilt. Our partners know they have done something wrong, but there's nothing tangible to which they can respond. I have discovered in my practice that most "it" statements are perceived as criticism and are very rarely responded to or even checked for meaning. Examples are:

"It hurt me when you showed up so late last night."

"It doesn't matter."

"It would be nice if you'd be home on time tonight."

"It's not much fun staying home all weekend."

As I hope you can see, these statements are more likely to elicit silent guilt than empathic/supportive listening. *Passive statements elicit passive responses.* Whenever we use a passive statement of this kind, we put ourselves down and lower our self-esteem. "It" statements, because of the assumption of criticism, are often seen as passive-aggressive.

FPs, especially when they are also introverted, like Fran, are most likely to use "it" statements. They are afraid to provoke conflict and yet, by avoiding conflict, they are the least likely to have their needs met in a relationship.

"YOU" STATEMENTS

Now let's look at "you" statements. These statements are seen as aggressive and will almost always prompt a defensive response. SJs, like Bob and Ed, are most likely to use them, especially when under stress. A statement that begins with "You . . ." will start an argument 90% of the time:

Bob: You never put your magazines away.

Annie: Well, you can talk. Whenever you have a snack, you leave everything out on the kitchen counter.

"You" statements blame your partner in one way or another and your partner will react to this blame defensively. This type of approach also gives our partners responsibility for our feelings:

Ed: You make me so mad when you stay in bed all morning.

Fran: Why shouldn't I stay in bed if I want to? I'm not stopping you doing anything.

Fran refuses to take responsibility for Ed's feelings in this case. And her response is not friendly; responses to "you" statements rarely are. Again, we feel powerless when we use them, as we are giving all responsibility for our mood to our partner. Every time we use aggressive statements we lower our self-esteem another notch.

"I" STATEMENTS

So now we're back to "I" statements, which have many advantages when you can get over the fear of using them. When you start a sentence with "I" there is no confusion, grammatically, about the first person subject of the sentence. Also there can be no argument that you don't know how you feel or think. You do not put blame on your partner, and consequently you're much less likely to elicit a defensive response. You sound clear and confident so you're less likely to be ignored. If you are afraid of seeming selfish or pushy, you can always ask for your partner's opinion or thoughts on the subject:

Annie: I'd like to go out to dinner Friday night. What do you want to do?

Bob: I've got a horrible day Friday and won't get home 'til seven. How about we rent a movie Friday night and go out Saturday?

Annie: Let me think about that.

Or,

Bob: I'd like us to have supper earlier and organize ourselves a bit better so that we can spend some time together in the evening after the kids are in bed. What do you think?

Annie: I agree. How are we going to do that?

A good exercise to do as a couple is to list all your complaints about each other on a piece of paper. Then change each complaint to a wish and share it with your partner:

Change

You never tell me what you are doing.

To

I'd like you to let me know what your plans are a bit in advance.

Or

You never suggest things to do together.

To

I'd like you to suggest something to do together once a month.

Or

You're always talking to your friends on the phone.

To

I'd like us to have some time to talk together in the evening (or, I'd like to read the paper/watch TV in peace).

Whenever we use "I" statements, we are assertive and feel confident. We raise our self-esteem a notch.

BE SPECIFIC

If you want to be clear, then make sure your message is complete and specific in detail. This means that you must include all the information your partner needs to understand what you have to say. For some reason, perhaps because we are afraid of being picky, it is very difficult to be specific. It seems so much easier, though not productive, to attack. Instead of saying, "I'd like you to pick up your socks from the bedroom floor," we are far more likely to say, "You're so messy," "You never clean up," or even, if feeling especially nasty, "You live like a pig." These latter statements are sure to start an argument and the socks, not having been mentioned, will stay on the floor.

Along the same lines, phrases that begin, "You always" or "You never" will also be ineffective. Your partner will inevitably be able to find times when he or she did not behave that way and you then lose credibility. "Always" and "never" statements are particularly self-defeating if you are living with an ST. They react badly to unfair statements and will usually win the ensuing argument. However many times the event has happened, it's much easier to deal with if you mention only the last one or two instances (more only if you are on very solid ground). Instead of "You're never on time," say instead, "You've been late every night this week." Both of you now know what you're dealing with and can address the problem:

Bob: The last three times I've come up to talk to you, you've been on the phone.

Annie: Yeah, I know. As soon as I put the phone down, it rang again. What did you want to say?

Rather than:

Bob: You're always talking on the phone.

Annie: No I'm not. This is only the third call all evening.

When you have addressed one issue successfully, you may be tempted to bring up another while you are on a roll. *Don't* go that route:

Annie: I asked you twice yesterday to take out the compost and I noticed it's still full. I thought we'd agreed that you'd do that.

Bob: You're right. I'll go and do it as soon as the commercials come on.

Annie: And you said last week that you'd fix the bathroom tap. It's still dripping.

Bob: I said I'd put out the compost. Aren't I going to get any peace this evening?

Be satisfied if you manage to resolve one issue satisfactorily.

BE CONGRUENT

Being congruent means that our verbal and non-verbal messages are the same. In order to get a clear message across, the words that we say have to match the image our bodies present. Often feelings that have little to do with the content of what we have to say interfere with the messages we want to convey.

For example, if Annie is angry with Bob, she may feel justified in her anger and strongly feel the need to express that anger before it builds up to resentment. So far, so good. However, Annie learned, as she was growing up, that anger is not attractive in a woman and is associated with such labels as "bitch" or "ball-breaker." This affects how she presents her anger bodily.

The words come out right:

Annie: I felt very angry when you made fun of my mother in front of Jo and Kate last night.

However, because of previous social conditioning, Annie smiles as she speaks so as to make the statement gentler and more feminine. As soon as she smiles, Bob gets the message that she's not really angry and pays little attention to the statement. If you want your message to be heard accurately and you are angry, you will need to look angry, or at least serious.

Something similar can happen to men when they find themselves in the scary realm of expressing emotion. Bob wants to express to Annie that he realizes he hurt her by his behaviour and feels very sorry about that. However, he learned when he was growing up not to express his feelings and that admitting to being in the wrong would put him "one down"—a position a male should never be in.

The words come out right:

Bob: I realize I hurt you by making fun of your mum like that and I'm really sorry.

However, because of Bob's social conditioning, he is embarrassed at the weakness of his position and is unable to look at Annie as he speaks. Annie takes his inability to look her in the eye as lack of sincerity, and his message is lost to her.

CHECK OUT WHAT YOU HEARD

When our partners do not respond to our messages the way we expect, it is important to check out what happened:

Annie: (smiling) I felt very angry when you made fun of my mother in front of Jo and Kate last night.

Bob: (laughing) Yeah, I know, but your mum's so funny.

Annie: I just said I was angry with you and you laughed. I feel like I'm not being taken seriously.

Bob: Oh, I didn't realize you were serious. I thought you were laughing about it too.

Or

Bob: (looking away) I realize I hurt you by making fun of your mum like that and I'm really sorry.

Annie: You just don't care!

Bob: I apologize to you for making fun of your mom and you get mad at me. What happened?

Annie: You didn't look at me when you said it. I didn't think you were being sincere.

When you have a difficult message to convey, make sure your body language is in sync with what you say. Otherwise you may get an unexpected response. If this happens, check it out. This is simple to do and may avoid many hours of bad feeling.

Sometimes we send a non-verbal signal unbeknownst to ourselves. Cathy and Dave as judging and perceptive types might get into this difficulty, as Cathy is quick to jump to conclusions. For example, Cathy might start talking to Dave while he is reading the newspaper. Quite absorbed in his newspaper and oblivious to Cathy's presence, Dave does not even look up. Cathy, upset by Dave's lack of response, leaves the room feeling hurt and angry. Dave later puts down his paper and goes in search of Cathy to ask her something and is greeted with anger. Dave may then withdraw, feeling either hurt, angry or both, wondering what he did this time. At this point, instead of withdrawing, Dave might check out what happened:

Dave: I came to ask you what time we were going out this evening and you snarled that I should figure it out for myself. What happened?

Cathy: Well, I came into the living room to talk to you and you completely ignored me. I don't think that was very friendly, either.

Dave: When did you do that? I don't remember you talking to me in the living room.

Cathy: That's because you were so absorbed in your newspaper!

Dave: Well, yeah, I guess I was absorbed in the paper and didn't hear you. I wouldn't just ignore you.

Cathy: Oh.

DESCRIBE RATHER THAN INTERPRET BEHAVIOUR

Often, when we don't like how our partners are behaving, we make a judgment call. We decide we know what the behaviour means and act accordingly. IFs are often likely to read non-verbal signals and act on them. In general, these types are very good at interpreting body language. However, in couple relationships they are quite likely to get it wrong. Judging types, often quick to make decisions without much data, may also misinterpret body language. In our cast of characters, Cathy, who has all three traits, would be most likely to interpret, and perhaps misinterpret, body language.

When Dave did not respond to Cathy while he was reading the newspaper, she assumed she knew what this behaviour meant and responded accordingly. This kind of assumption seems to be universal to all couple relationships. However, a good deal of the time we are wrong. Even when we get it right, it is not constructive to share it. This almost always elicits a defensive response. It is far more productive to share what we see rather than what we think we see. Anyone who has read a parenting book will read that as a parent it is far more constructive to criticize the behaviour than the child. Well, this is true for adults, too. If you describe what you actually see, you are on far more solid ground than if you confront your partner with what you think he/she is thinking or feeling:

Cathy: You are reading the paper while I am talking to you.

Rather than

You're ignoring me.

Or

You're obviously not interested in what I have to say.

Even when there is no doubt in your mind as to what the non-verbal signals mean, it is still not productive to share that perception—your partner will almost certainly deny it. Human beings do not seem to take kindly to someone telling them how they feel. Perhaps it is perceived as an invasion of privacy. For whatever the reason, defense or attack is usually the response:

Bob: What are you so mad about?

Annie: I'm not mad. What are you talking about?

Or the classic:

Annie: What's the matter?

Bob: Nothing.

In my experience, "What's the matter?" is nearly always heard as, "What's the matter now?" and is subsequently perceived as criticism.

More constructive in this case is to describe the behaviour that gives rise to this assumption:

Bob: You slammed the door and didn't look at me when you came in. Is something wrong?

Annie: Yes. I just tripped over the garbage you were supposed to put out this morning!

Or:

Annie: You're looking a bit down. Are you okay?

Bob: No. I just heard there are going to be more layoffs next week.

If you're upset about your partner's behaviour, switch off the analytical side of your brain and stay with what you observe. You will gain far more credibility in your partner's eyes.

SO HOW DO YOU PUT THIS ALL TOGETHER?

You now have some pretty solid rules for communicating directly. However, many clients have said to me that they see the relevance of all these rules, but are not sure how they are supposed to remember them all when they're in the middle of a tricky situation, or are so overcome with emotion that their brains aren't in gear. The first thing to remember when you are changing communication patterns is that you are unlikely to get it right the first time. The first step is awareness, and if you are aware that you are not speaking constructively you can stop mid-stream, back up, and start again. No, you will not lose credibility if you do this. If you started out wrong, you've already lost credibility; so you can only gain. In the following section we will look at a model you can use as a guideline with which to begin.

A MODEL OF ASSERTIVE COMMUNICATION

Books on assertive communication suggest variations of the following model that my clients have found useful for "putting it all together":

When you . . . (describe the behaviour you see in a specific way and without assuming a motive)

I feel . . . (state how you feel and/or the effect this may have on you)

I would like you to . . . instead (suggest an alternative behaviour).

Or

Would you be willing to . . . instead?

For example:

Annie: When you read the newspaper while I'm talking to you, I feel unimportant (statement of feeling). I'd like you to put the newspaper down while I'm talking to you.

Or

Bob: When you talk to me while I am reading the newspaper, I can't concentrate on what I'm reading (statement of effect). I'd like you to wait 'til I've finished reading the paper before talking to me.

At the beginning, these statements may feel belaboured and unnatural. That is probably because you are not used to being that specific and direct. Listen to small children communicating if you want a good model. They are usually very direct and specific.

You can also use this model to give positive feedback. However, in this case leave out the request for change, as this alters the positive statement to what is usually perceived as a criticism:

Annie: When you rub my back I feel great.

Or

Bob: I really appreciate you cooking my favourite dessert.

I'm sure you can see that if Bob or Annie had added, "I wish you'd do it more often," then the positive affirmation would be lost.

You may be more comfortable putting the feeling first, especially when giving positive affirmations. This can also work well. However, if you are angry, annoyed or irritated, your partner will probably be more at ease if you start with what happened and then express how you feel/felt about it.

So now you have the basics of good communication. In the next chapter we will look at how to apply these skills in specific situations related to conflict and criticism.

CHAPTER 7

Dealing with Anger and Criticism

Expressing and dealing with anger and criticism are very difficult for couples. Historically, only the male was allowed to express anger in a couple relationship, and in a traditional marriage the wife would rarely retaliate. If she did, and sometimes even if she didn't, it was quite acceptable for the husband to use physical means to back up the complaint. During the transition years, while men and women were finding their footing with their new roles and in their new environments, relationships were difficult, and anger and criticism were often expressed inappropriately.

When couples did resolve their differences appropriately, there was a rule that stated "not in front of the children," so that children never saw their parents having arguments and resolving them. For whatever the reason, the majority of couples now have no positive models for resolving negative feelings.

The fact that we rarely saw differences handled in a constructive manner has given rise to a number of beliefs that vary according to what model of negative communication we were brought up with. If you grew up in a home where negative feelings were dealt with in a violent or disrespectful way, you might have the following beliefs:

- I'll be seen as a monster if I express negative feelings.
- I might lose control if I express negative feelings.
- He/she will retaliate if I express how I feel.
- I'll look like a complete idiot if I get angry.
- I'll be behaving just like my mom/dad if I get mad.
- He/she will hit me if I get mad.
- He/she will make fun of me if I get mad.
- He/she will walk out on me if I get mad.

If you were brought up in a home where all conflict was discussed behind closed doors, these might be some of your beliefs:

- Good relationships don't have any conflict.
- If we can't agree, we can't really be suited to each other.
- I should try and resolve my conflicts by talking to friends or therapists.
- There must be something wrong with me or with him/her if I'm angry with him/her, or he/she is angry with me.
- If you don't have something nice to say then keep quiet.
- I should never get mad.

As you can see from reading both lists, all these beliefs will prohibit you from saying what's on your mind. What happens instead is one of two things: either we say nothing and build up such a strong resentment that we become distant from our partners and cease to want to relate to them at all; or we say nothing until we can't contain our feelings any longer and the whole lot comes out at once—usually in a destructive, disrespectful way.

Family history often determines which strategies we use to deal with our angry feelings. What did expression of anger mean in our original families? What we learned as kids tends to affect not only our beliefs but also how we behave as adults.

If you were brought up in a family that dealt with anger by not expressing it out loud, then your strategy will probably be to repress anger and pretend it's not there. You might also ignore your partner's anger. You might tell your partner that there is something wrong with him/her and he/she had better shape up. The presence of angry feelings in you or your partner is threatening to your belief that couples in healthy relationships don't feel or express negative emotions. Often, in this case, the understanding that anger is a permitted emotion and the learning of a few communication techniques are all you need to deal comfortably with the conflict.

If you were brought up in a family whose parents dealt with anger in a violent/submissive manner, then how you deal with it now will depend upon which parent you identify with, and which coping mechanism you choose. If you identify with the violent parent, you might become violent yourself. Alternatively, you could be very much afraid that you might be violent and consequently will feel unable to express your anger at all for fear of this monster in you. If you identify with the submissive parent, you might become submissive yourself, or be so afraid of being dominated that you become super-aggressive in order to protect yourself.

If you were brought up in a family where both parents were aggressive and violent and you witnessed a lot of fighting as you were growing up, then in general your strategy may be to avoid anger at all costs—both your own and your partner's. This approach will lead you to repress your own anger for as long as you can and deny your partner's expression of anger. Nothing must ever allow your own relationship to follow in the footsteps of your parents.

Not one of the above three scenarios will help to foster an intimate, caring relationship.

All the above strategies make the assumption that as soon as anger is expressed, you are in a position with no control, neither over your response to your partner's anger nor your own anger. You are suddenly driving a car with no brakes and no steering wheel. When you are in that position you will do anything that gives you a semblance of control. You are not at your creative best for problem solving. As soon as anger is in the air, the strategies are set and acted out so as to give you a feeling of being in control.

This is an illusion. If you are behaving in this way, you are being controlled by habits learned in the past that have no relevance in the present.

Unless you are in a violent relationship with a physically abusive partner, you can deal with conflict *and* remain in control *if you choose to do so.* **The belief that you can control both how you behave and how you respond to your partner's behaviour is a crucial one for an honest, intimate relationship.** When you believe you are in control, you will feel safe enough to use the following strategies for expressing and dealing with anger.

If you are in an abusive relationship, then you may well be endangered if you assert yourself honestly, and you may want to question whether this relationship is worth that.

So, before we can even begin to look at ways to express or deal with conflict, we have to tell ourselves that it is okay and healthy to do so. When two different people live together, if they are to remain individuals, there will be some conflict. As long as you can talk about it in a respectful manner, things are unlikely to get out of control. If they do, you can take time out and look at the conflict again later.

Let's look at anger first.

EXPRESSING ANGRY FEELINGS

Expressing angry feelings is easy if you use the model described at the end of Chapter 6.

The important thing to remember as you begin to express anger is that it will be constructive only if you communicate with respect. This is important to keep in mind, because being respectful is the last thing we think of when we are angry. Since anger is such a fearful emotion, you may still get a defensive response even when you use an "I" statement. If you get a defensive response, you may need to refocus attention on what you want to say:

Bob: When you told Mark he could watch TV after I'd said he couldn't, I felt really mad. I'd like you to back up my decisions in front of the kids.

Annie: Well, you don't always back my decisions. Last Christmas you let them go out skating when I'd said they couldn't.

Bob: We're not talking about what I did last Christmas; we can talk about that later. I'd like to talk about how I felt today and what we can do to ensure it doesn't happen again.

When we are angry, it is important that our body language says that, too. As stated earlier, we can lose our point immediately if we smile or joke or put ourselves down as we speak. Some people, especially FPs, try to soften their anger by prefacing their complaints with comments such as, "I know I'm being picky/stupid/silly but I get really mad when . . . " You don't need to put yourself down when you express negative feelings. If you do, you won't be treated seriously and you will have wasted your time.

If you find that you are too angry to confront the situation in a constructive way, give yourself some time to calm down. You don't have to respond immediately, and you will be more effective if you are calm. Take some deep breaths and get some balance in your thinking. You may want to say to yourself something like, "This is just one situation," or, "He/she is not a bad person," or, "When we've resolved this, things will be okay again." However, don't rationalize your anger away in this breathing space. This is a time for extroverts to behave like introverts: think for a moment before speaking. Ensure that what you are about to say is constructive.

When we are learning to communicate differently, we may often lapse into bad habits. Especially when we are angry, we may feel the desire to punish our partners for causing us distress and may blame them. While this is a perfectly natural way to feel, it is not constructive to act it out. If we do this, we will get into a fight and we'll end up feeling even worse. So, if you start off on the wrong foot, for example, with a "you" statement, backtrack and start again. Forgive yourself for not getting it right the first time—at least you're trying!

If you are angry and want to sort it out, give yourself enough time to do so. Choosing to express your anger just as your partner is leaving home in the morning is not a good time, nor is it the best moment just as you collapse into bed at night. Often when we are angry, we will decide to express our feelings at the most inappropriate time, perhaps to have an excuse if it doesn't work. Choose a time when you are both available to talk about your feelings. The kids can be present if the issue is appropriate for them.

DEALING WITH OUR PARTNER'S ANGER

When you are on the receiving end of your partner's anger, a rather different strategy applies than when you express your own. It is actually a far better idea **not** to think too much. At the receiving end of anger you need to switch off the part of the brain that analyzes, problem solves, thinks of excuses, justifies, or simply searches around for something to be angry back about. The most effective way to calm anger, especially accusing or blaming anger, is simply to paraphrase what you hear back to your partner:

Bob: You're not ready again when it's time to leave! You're only ever on time when it's something you want to do. You obviously don't care about me at all.

Annie: You're saying that I'm not ready again and this only happens when it's something you want to do and it must mean that I don't care about you at all?

When you repeat the facts as heard back to your partner, you have decided not to get involved in an argument. When you state the facts back calmly, you change the tone of the interaction to be less heated. A calmer, non-combative interaction is more likely to lead to a constructive solution than a heated fight. **You can't have a battle if one side isn't fighting.** Most often when we hear our unfair blaming statements repeated back to us, we realize they are not quite what we mean and we are willing to express them in a fairer manner.

Your angry partner may not always appreciate your paraphrasing. This technique is more self-protecting than partner-protecting. If it doesn't work, you may need to take a "time out," stating that you will talk about it again later when he/she has calmed down.

TPs, like John and Dave, generally deal with anger by becoming ultra-reasonable. They want to avoid conflict at all costs and believe that a logical solution, stated in a calm manner, will resolve the conflict. This may sometimes work for John, as Iris is also a thinking type. However it will not work for Dave, as Cathy is a feeling type. She is likely to become even angrier in response to this approach, with John's logic only serving to increase Cathy's emotional response. An empathic, listening response will be far more effective.

Paraphrasing is also effective when the anger is expressed to us in a respectful manner. We inform our partners that we are listening to their feelings and at the same time give ourselves breathing space to get over our own discomfort. Often, the space to express anger uncontested, and have it listened to, are all the angry person needs to feel better. If you want your partner to get over his/her anger so that you can get on with your lives, the first thing to do is listen to the anger as it is expressed. When you have listened to the content, validate the feeling with statements such as: "I can see that you're really upset about that," and, if appropriate, "I'm sorry I did that. I'll try and be more careful next time." It is never effective to meet anger with anger. If you are angry too, then wait for another occasion to express your feeling.

If you find that you are feeling scared or intimidated by your partner's body language, then point that out while also recognizing the angry feeling:

Annie: I understand that you're mad at me. However, when you shout and point your finger at me, I get scared. Please lower your voice and keep your hands still.

GOALS OF EXPRESSING AND RECEIVING ANGRY FEELINGS

When we want to express our anger, the goals we have are usually fairly simple:

- to let go of our anger
- to feel better
- to have some assurance that whatever happened won't happen again

- to feel close to our partners again
- to get on with the rest of the day

When we are on the receiving end of our partners' anger, again the goals are simple:

- to help our partners get over their anger
- to have both of us feeling better
- to know what to do so it won't happen again
- to feel close to our partners again
- to get on with the rest of our day

When we are expressing anger or are on the receiving end, we need to be very conscious of our goals and avoid behaviours that will handicap these goals.

BEHAVIOURS THAT WILL SABOTAGE OUR GOALS

- shouting
- threatening body language
- walking out without saying that you'll be back later when your partner is calmer
- blaming
- accusing (especially of being over-emotional)
- labelling
- meeting anger with anger
- insulting
- sarcasm
- lack of eye contact
- incongruent body language

If you find yourself using any of the above behaviours, watch out! Things will escalate to a war before you know it—a war that might take days to end.

In an ideal world, the partner expressing anger would start off right; in reality, this does not often happen. When it doesn't happen, then it is up to the receiver to take charge of where the interaction is going, as he or she is less emotionally involved at the start. At any point, either one can request time out until both are calmer. **Remember: both of you can be in control if you decide to be.**

In the next section I will look at techniques for dealing with criticism. This is dealt with separately from the section on anger, although the techniques may well be useful too when the angry part is over and a problem-solving stage is needed. The difference between dealing with anger and dealing with criticism is that when our partners are angry it may not have anything to do with our behaviour, whereas when they are critical it usually does—although not always the behaviour that is under discussion.

DEALING WITH CRITICISM

The perception of criticism and the lack of ability to deal with it comfortably or constructively may well be the major difficulty in relationships. As mentioned in Chapter 6, when we are upset with our partners, our natural instinct is to lash out at them and lay blame. When we are on the receiving end of this, our natural instinct is to withdraw or fight back. Neither of these behaviours is conducive to a loving relationship. Most criticisms that are not well thought out begin with a "you" statement. Probably the most common criticisms start with "You always . . ." or "You never . . ."

Sensing-judging types, when under stress, are the most likely to use blaming statements. If you are hearing a lot of these statements from your sensing-judging partner, it is a clue that he or she is stressed for some reason. This may be worth investigating.

When you are on the receiving end of a criticism that starts with a "you" statement, the first thing to remember is that **this blaming statement is covering an "I" statement.** Your goal as a listener is to discover what it is. I have found, in my practice, that most blaming criticisms cover a very small range of "I" sentiments:

- I am feeling lonely.
- I am feeling rejected.

- I am feeling worried about something.
- I was feeling worried about you.
- I feel unimportant in your life.

For some reason, these things are very difficult to say; perhaps the critical partner feels too vulnerable and so he/she armours him/herself with fighting gear. Unfortunately, when this happens, the issue originally brought up with the blaming statement is the one addressed, and often not in a caring way. The real issue is never acknowledged.

The goal of the following two techniques is to discover the hidden "I" message.

CHECKING IT OUT

When we use this technique, our first aim is to ensure that a criticism was meant in the first place. This response is useful for criticism that is indirect and perceived as passive-aggressive:

Annie: Dinner is taking a long time to prepare.

Bob: Are you saying that I should have finished preparing dinner by now?

Annie: Yes, I was hoping dinner would be ready by now. I have to leave in half an hour and I wanted to eat before I left.

Bob's "checking out" question is able to elicit an "I" statement from Annie and he now has far more useful information with which to work. It was important to check the meaning of Annie's indirect statement. Her statement could have many meanings and not all of them critical:

Annie: Dinner is taking a long time to prepare.

Bob: Are you saying that I should have finished preparing dinner by now?

Annie: No, I was just wondering if you might like some help. There seems to be a lot to do.

Or

Annie: Dinner is taking a long time to prepare.

Bob: Are you saying that I should have finished preparing dinner by now?

Annie: No, I realize it's special and will take a long time to prepare. I'm just feeling disappointed because we won't have much time to relax and enjoy it before the kids come home. Are you sure you don't want some help?

Whenever you hear a statement that is ambiguous—maybe critical, maybe not, or even when you are sure that it is a veiled criticism—check it out. If it was not meant as a criticism, then you have prevented an uncomfortable situation from developing. If it was meant as a criticism, then you have prompted your partner to be more assertive, which will boost his/her self-esteem and benefit you in the end. You will also encourage your partner to use more direct statements to start with.

FINDING OUT WHAT BLAMING CRITICISM IS REALLY ABOUT

As mentioned earlier, blaming criticism usually covers a difficulty with assertiveness on the critic's part. If our goal on the receiving end is to discover what the criticism is really about, then supportive questioning will work well. Manuel Smith, in his book entitled *When I Say No I Feel Guilty*, suggested a useful technique called negative inquiry. He suggested this technique as a means to promote direct, open and honest communication with those closest to us. Again, it is much easier to use this technique if we can ignore the part of our brain that wants to fight back and, instead, stay with the goal of becoming close again in our relationship. These criticisms usually start with a "you" statement like this example from Cathy and Dave:

Cathy: All you ever do is play hockey!

Dave: What is it about my playing hockey so much that bothers you?

Cathy: I'd like us to do something together once in a while.

This time, an "I" statement came quickly. This is not always the case:

Cathy: All you ever do is play hockey!

Dave: What is it about my playing hockey so much that bothers you?

Annie: You're never home!

Dave: So what is it about my not being home that bothers you?

Cathy: You're never here to watch the kids!

Dave: So what is it about my not being here to watch the kids that bothers you?

Cathy: I'd like to go out sometimes. I feel my needs aren't important to you.

As you can see, in this instance it took a long time to get to the point. You may think this is very tedious, and you are right. However, if you don't get through to this end point, you will still be arguing about hockey and not looking at how to balance both your and your partner's social needs. If you persist with a questioning response to "you" statements, you will find that your partner will also get bored with this process and will start being assertive much sooner. A side bonus for this type of response to blaming is that it gives us a clear goal to work toward—getting the "I" statement—that distracts us from the more immediate wish to give a more defensive response. I have found that this technique works best if you explain to your partner that this is the way you will respond to all blaming in the future. Both of you then know what is going on, and this can make the whole process much easier. I have found that, when I work with couples on this technique in my office, they often end up laughing together. This lightens the mood considerably.

ADMITTING WHEN WE ARE IN THE WRONG

When it is clear that you are in the wrong, it is actually much simpler to admit the fact than to come up with some counter-argument or justification. At least, finding the words is much easier. Unfortunately our belief systems get in the way again. Two beliefs are predominant in this case:

- I should be perfect.
- If I'm not perfect, then I'm a bad person and should feel guilty about it.

We need to change our belief that we must be perfect. We know rationally that we are not, and will have little difficulty acknowledging it out of context. However, when we are confronted with our imperfection, our first response is often to defend ourselves or to counter-attack. **Paraphrasing can be useful here, as it gives you something to say immediately while you are dealing with the programmed messages going through your mind.** Phrases that validate the feeling can also be helpful:

Bob: I feel really frustrated when you interrupt me while I'm working on the computer.

Annie: I understand you find my interrupting really frustrating.

Once Annie has got the messages in her head sorted out and replaced with:

- It's okay to make mistakes.
- He doesn't hate me, he just didn't like what I did.
- I'm not a bad person for getting this wrong.
- I can apologize and move on.

Then she is ready to finish up:

Bob: I feel really frustrated when you interrupt me while I'm working on the computer.

Annie: I understand you find my interrupting really frustrating. I'm sorry to have disturbed you. I'll wait until you are finished.

It's important to keep your tone of voice in line with your intent. It is sometimes tempting to use a sarcastic tone of voice. What would be the point of doing that? Is it worth it?

There will be times when you may need to stick to your behaviour even when criticized. This is fine, but validate the feeling first:

Bob: I feel really frustrated when you interrupt me while I'm working on the computer.

Annie: I understand you find my interrupting really frustrating. However, this is important. The school just phoned to say that Mark isn't at school today. Do you have any idea where he might be?

HUMOUR AND CONFLICT

Taking a humourous approach can sometimes lighten conflict, if the conflict is not too serious. Finding the funny side of an argument that is in progress may prevent it from getting out of control. Playful sensing or intuitive-feeling-perceptive types like Annie, Fran or Leo are especially good at this. Be careful, however, not to laugh at or make fun of your partner. This will only serve to aggravate the situation.

PERSONALITY AND CONFLICT

STJs, like Ed and Bob, often have difficulty seeing the other point of view in a conflict. Ed gathers all the evidence (S) and makes a decision (J) based on logic (T). He sees decisions as being right or wrong. Fran has little evidence to back her decisions, which are based on her interpretation of the data (N) and the impact on the individuals concerned (F). When faced with Ed's certainty, she usually backs down and this, over time, becomes very damaging to the relationship (see Chapter 4). A couple's conflict is one of those situations where there can be two conflicting perspectives that are both correct.

Other individuals may be equally decisive but base their decisions on different criteria. SFJs also have a different perspective to the STJ's; they use the same data and are just as decisive, but they are likely to include a consideration of the people concerned (F). INTJs also use logic as a basis, but in addition they will take into account their unique interpretation of the data.

As you can see, there are many different ways of reaching decisions and all of them can be "right" within a given context. The sensing and thinking combination tend to deliver a particularly powerful argument, and partners of STJs, especially when they are ESTJs, often back down in the face of such strong opposition. However, they will not be comfortable with having to back down and may, over time, withdraw, feeling that their opinions are not valued.

A logically correct solution is not always the best way to go. People considerations are important, too. If you live in a relationship with opposite personality traits, you will need to ensure that both styles are being heard and respected, and acted on at least occasionally.

To end this chapter on dealing with conflict, I'll suggest some rules that may be useful for a fair and intimacy-building conclusion to your conflict. You may want to add some of your own.

RULES FOR FIGHTING FAIR

- Communicate with respect for yourself and your partner.
- **Do not ever use physical means** to make your point or vent your frustration when you are not understood.
- State specifically only what you can observe and know to be true.
- Apologize when appropriate.
- Avoid aggressive body language and tone of voice.
- Avoid "you" and "it" statements. Take ownership of your feelings with "I" statements.
- Don't insult, label or swear at your partner.
- Choose a good time for discussion of differences.
- Stop for a "time out" if things become too heated.
- Avoid words like "always," "never" and "should."
- **Remember your ultimate goal.**

If you can keep the last rule in mind, all the rest will come more easily.

This completes the section of the book that focuses on particular communication skills. I would like next to look at some areas of communication that are particularly tricky. In my experience of working with couples, it appears that the same issues crop up again and again to create a challenge for even the best communicators. We will look at some of those in the next and final chapter.

Chapter 8

Difficult Communication Issues

In this last chapter, I will discuss a few especially difficult issues. While I do not intend to go into any detail on specific areas—that is not the domain of this book—it is useful at least to highlight a few areas where communication in couple relationships tends to break down. My purpose here is to share this information so that you will feel less alone. If you know that these are typical problems, then you may realize that your relationship is not worse than anyone else's.

Individuals rarely share all that is going on in their relationships. If you spent your childhood in a particularly bad family environment, you may well believe that other families were perfect and didn't have any of the difficulties your family was experiencing. If you spent your childhood in a happy family environment, where difficulties and arguments were never aired in front of the children, you may also believe that most families run smoothly. When you don't share what's happening in your relationship, you will not find out what the reality is for most people. Couples who are both introverted, like Greg and Helen, may be vulnerable to this kind of isolation.

Dissatisfaction with the modern relationship may, in part, be related to the presentation of relationships in the media. The media has never focused on the day-to-day functioning of a comfortable partnership—that would be too boring! Instead, they are portrayed as constantly exciting: either wonderful or awful, but never in the middle. We are beginning to realize that television viewing and exposure to other media affects our children's values; maybe we adults are also influenced.

The four main areas of conflict that seem to come up over and over again in relationships are:

- sexual intimacy
- finances
- social time
- chores

The above four areas quickly translate to the following faulty assumptions:

- If we don't have sex as often as I would like, then it means my partner doesn't love me.
- If my partner doesn't pay attention to my worries about overspending, then it means he/she doesn't love me.
- If my partner doesn't talk to me, then it means he/she doesn't love me.
- If my partner doesn't help with the housework, then it means he/she doesn't love me.

Conflict is much easier to deal with if we don't make these assumptions.

Issues of conflict often come together in pairs. For example, one individual might be distressed by an unsatisfying sexual relationship while the other is concerned with the lack of time spent talking together. Let's look at the area of sexual intimacy first.

HOW OFTEN SHOULD WE BE SEXUALLY INTIMATE?

Couples ask this question again and again. How many times should we be having sex? What's normal? What's wrong with him or her that he or she wants it more or less? Sexual relationships have come out into the open and now everyone is comparing their experiences with everyone else's. The answer to this question is easy, although it is not always acceptable. The normal relationship for you as a couple is the one that you negotiate between you, the one that most suits the two of you. Sexual interest is different from one individual to the next; and the sex drive of males and females seems to fluctuate at various points in their lives. We will look at a typical pattern, using Annie and Bob as an example.

Annie and Bob got married in their mid-twenties after knowing each other for a few years. They decided to get married because both were interested in having children. Very soon they were a family of four.

In the early years of their marriage, Annie found that her sex drive was low. She rarely got a good night's sleep and often felt overwhelmed by all the extra responsibility. She felt constantly tired and had little extra energy. Annie put on weight and no longer felt good about her body shape. Whenever she had spare time, she wanted to talk to Bob about her worries, or sleep, or escape with a good book.

Bob, however, was not in sync with Annie at all sexually. He felt stressed with all the extra responsibility and a little left out of the strong bond that Annie had with the two children. He wanted to express his caring and his connection with Annie by making love.

Unfortunately, Annie began to view Bob's sexual demands as another burden in her life. She felt angry that he did not understand that she was far too tired to look after him, too. She had difficulty talking about this for fear of hurting his feelings; and so distance between them developed. Annie ceased being affectionate with Bob for fear he would carry it further than she found comfortable. Bob, feeling rejected, began to find things to do that took him away from Annie, either spending more time at work or on projects that kept him away from home or Annie's company. Bob's absence and preoccupation distressed her, and so the distance widened.

For many couples, this destructive pattern that often develops in the early stages of marriage takes many years to mend. Both feel rejected and neither talks about it, fearing that confronting the problem might put the relationship in jeopardy. Eventually, most couples that stay together address the situation when the kids are older and there are fewer demands on their time. But do they need to wait that long?

Making love, when both partners are in the mood, is an experience that is enriching and intimacy-building. When Annie lost touch with her sexual side, Bob tried to keep this fun, playful side of the relationship alive. Once Annie was able to interpret Bob's efforts in this way, she was better able to see his behaviour as caring for her, rather than pestering her to meet his own needs. The next step was for her to express her own needs more effectively. Often her difficulty had been in establishing her boundaries: it was better to have no physical contact at all than to have to say, "I don't feel like going any further just now."

This difficulty with boundaries is partly cultural. Women are raised to please men and many have been raised with no model of womanly assertiveness. They don't have the words to assert their boundaries and are often not sure they have permission to do so. The result is often a sudden leap from passivity to aggression, and their male partners have no idea where this has come from. The key here is to deal with the rejection at the same time as establishing the boundaries.

Bob: You're pulling away from me again!

Annie: I do want to be close to you, but I'm feeling too tired to make love right now. I hope I'll feel more relaxed on the weekend.

If Bob shows disappointment, then Annie can empathize with his reaction:

Annie: I know it's a drag. I wish I had more energy, too.

This approach is far more constructive and effective than being offended by the disappointment.

As the children became older and more independent, Annie and Bob began to reconnect, and Annie began to see herself as a sexual being again. However, by this time, Bob had become heavily involved with his career. He was getting older and felt less secure in his work position. Recently, one of his staff had been offered a job over him. He felt that if he didn't work long hours he would lose his job and worried that he would not get another one at his age. This constant anxiety and long hours of work depleted Bob's energy and lessened his interest in sexual activity. At this stage, it is Annie's responsibility to keep the fun side of the relationship alive. Ironically, Bob may now need to learn to establish his sexual boundaries—something he never had an interest in doing before. Like Annie, Bob may need to learn to do this in a way that respects his partner's feelings of rejection.

Research in the male and female sexual response has demonstrated that men and women are rarely synchronized in their needs for sexual intimacy. Men often have difficulty expressing their love for their partners in words, and therefore sex is the chief way they express their commitment. It is very sad that their mates so often misinterpret this show of love and caring.

If you find that you and your partner are out of synch sexually and that this is causing a rift between you:

- Talk about how you feel. Talking is far less dangerous than silence.
- Be sensitive to your partner.
- Let him or her know that you are discussing this issue because you want to be closer, not because you want to criticize.
- Assume that you both care about the relationship.

A past history of physical and emotional pain related to sexual interaction will affect a person's sexual response even when the present relationship is a good one. Men and women who have been sexually abused as children, or in a chronically abusive relationship as an adult, may find it hard to respond to their partners. They will not usually define sexual interaction as a loving act but as a demeaning, painful one. Such individuals would benefit from a good therapist to help them come to terms with their past painful experiences. I have found that women who have had difficulty conceiving, perhaps experiencing many miscarriages, also tend to link sexual interaction with pain and disappointment and may have difficulty responding comfortably. In these cases, again, a therapist can be very helpful.

Personality differences, especially in the area of thinking/feeling, may also create confusion related to intimacy. Greg and Helen are a typical example. Greg, as a feeling type, enjoys a good deal of physical contact. He is constantly reaching out to Helen for physical reassurance that she loves him. Helen, however, is a thinking type. She is not comfortable with a lot of physical contact. Greg interprets this discomfort as a lack of caring and feels emotionally and sexually rejected. They need to discuss this difference and find a balance that is mutually comfortable.

Introverts and extroverts enjoy making love differently. Introverts enjoy the experience internally and are much more likely to close their eyes and remain quiet. Extroverts often want to enjoy the experience externally, with open eyes and verbal exchange. This works well when extroverts and introverts are with the same types, but if they are together in a relationship, they will need to negotiate quiet and interaction.

Now that we have looked at one major area of relationship conflict, let's move on to another: finances.

WHO SHOULD BE SPENDING HOW MUCH ON WHAT?

While sexual intimacy tends to be an area that couples avoid talking about, this is not generally true of their spending habits. Arguments are often heated and disrespectful in this area, because attitudes towards finances are usually based on the values they learned from their families; these are not easy to relinquish. Let's see how Annie and Bob fare in this area of their relationship.

Annie was the youngest in her family. By the time she was born, her family was well established financially and, being new to wealth, her parents were pleased to spoil their youngest daughter. Annie grew up getting most of the things she wanted. Her parents often went into debt, knowing they would be able to handle the payments.

Bob was the eldest in a family with four children. His mother stayed at home to look after the family and his father worked as a civil servant to support them. Bob's family was not well off, but his parents managed their money well and all the children were able to get a good education. His dad lost his job at one point and was out of work for a year. If they had still been paying for their house at that time they might have lost it.

Annie, as an ENFP, may sometimes be an impulsive spender. Bob, an ISTJ, is far more cautious. Their family backgrounds and personalities have given Bob and Annie completely different values with regard to spending.

Annie believed they both had good earning power even though she was not always working, so they would always be able to get themselves out of debt if they needed to. She thought they could save some money every month to put toward their children's education, but otherwise why not spend their money on the things they want now? She worried when her children didn't have the toys and clothes that other children had. They had plenty of time to pay off their mortgage.

Bob thought quite differently. They were able to make good money at that time, but who knows what the future will bring? He would have felt much more secure if they could have paid off their house quickly; then they would have had money to spend on themselves. He looked forward to an early retirement. His parents had very little when he was small and the kids were happy. He saw no need to buy his children expensive toys and clothes. Better that they learnt about the value of money.

Individuals from these different types of background often join together as couples. Each gains from the other's financial perspective. Annie gains from Bob's careful spending: they will never get seriously in debt, which maintains the family's financial security. Bob gains from Annie's willingness to spend money. She has created a comfortable home and will occasionally persuade Bob to go out for a nice meal or to the theatre. Unfortunately, however, neither appreciates the gifts each brings to the relationship. Their different spending habits cause constant conflict because each believes the other is wrong, and that a loving and caring partner would listen to and respect his/her partner's values. Neither of these beliefs is helpful to the situation.

Both perspectives on spending are valid. It is true that if you save money now and build for the future, you will probably have more security and may have the opportunity to retire early. It is also true that if you have good earning power, you can buy the things you want now and probably pay back any debt that you accumulate later. **Neither approach is wrong; they just don't work well together.** When partners recognize that both ways have their merits, it is much easier to find a middle ground.

Similarly, the assumption that not listening to each other's perspective on finances means a lack of love and respect is usually not correct. Our values generally come from our parents or other parental figures. If we bring these values into our new families, it means we believe in them and believe they worked well for our parents. When these convictions are challenged, we have not only to defend ourselves but our parents as well, who we may believe did an excellent job of raising us and keeping the family financially secure. We will not react calmly if we are informed that our values are ridiculous. The first and most important step in resolving the conflict is to listen respectfully to your partner's perspective and to understand its importance in his/her life. When both of you are able to listen respectfully, the next steps of problem solving and compromising are much easier.

HOW MUCH TIME SHOULD WE SPEND TOGETHER?

Another area that causes a considerable amount of distress is the amount of time spent together as a couple. While we looked at this area in the chapter on introverts and extroverts and how they require different amounts of personal space, culture is another factor that influences time spent together.

As discussed in the Introduction, men in the first part of the twentieth century were not expected to take much part in the social side of family life. If you ask many adults in today's baby boomer generation how much they saw their fathers, they will often say they were not at home much. They may remember them participating in important family occasions or holidays, but otherwise they were seen as the one who worked hard to keep the family afloat. Even today, it is not unusual to have fathers absent for long periods, either on business trips or on tours of duty if they are in the armed forces. Even the corporate culture of today—expecting longer and longer hours of work from its employees—does not recognize or respect the role of father and husband. Consequently, men do not have models of husbands and fathers who spend long periods of time socializing with their wives and children, and often do not understand why this would be expected of them. In their families they may have seen their parents spend time together only in their retirement years, and may be looking forward to spending time with their wives then, when their working years are over.

The first step in dealing with this issue as a couple is to avoid blaming your partner for the expectations that the corporate culture puts on its workers whether they are male or female. With unemployment and downsizing, employees are in constant fear of losing their jobs. This fear makes employees vulnerable to unreasonable demands from their employers. It takes a lot of courage to fight against something that provides one's livelihood. It is sometimes easier to handle unreasonable work demands if the couple has a common goal that is discussed and revised occasionally. If each knows that the other is working toward the same goal, both partners will feel like a team and will recognize each other's efforts.

WHO SHOULD DO WHICH HOUSEHOLD CHORES?

Household chores are often the subject of disharmony in a relationship. Again, the models that our parents offered us do not help to resolve the issue of division of household labour. Our parents did not typically have arguments about this. Chores were usually divided according to male-female expertise. Women did most of the indoor housework that did not require heavy physical labour. Men did most of the outside work and other indoor work that fell into the "male" domain, such as painting, building shelves, or repairing leaky pipes.

In Cathy and Dave's relationship, confusion about domestic roles emerged once Cathy started working. Although Cathy was working full time, she had little power in her work role; many women are still struggling for equal power and recognition in the workplace. Between the two of them, Cathy felt that she was the expert in running the family home. She had watched her mother running the home successfully and so understood well how to fill that role, and would notice right away when something needed to be done. Unfortunately, she did not have enough time to do a good job.

In Dave's family there had been no expectation that his father help around the house. His father did his work, came home and rested. Neither was Dave expected to help. Consequently, his mother had not passed on her domestic skills to him. Dave knew that he should help Cathy, but was not sure how. He did not feel confident in this area, but was uncomfortable confiding this unease to Cathy. While it was obvious to Cathy that something needed to be done, it was not so obvious to Dave. He also found it difficult to do things the way Cathy would expect.

Cathy and Dave need to identify household chores and agree on a fair division of labour. Once couples decide to do this, they generally have little difficulty coming up with a workable program. As children become older, they can be included in the chore schedule. Cathy may also have to change her standards in order to enlist Dave's help. Nobody feels like helping if his or her effort is likely to be criticized.

SJs generally run the most organized households. NPs are generally the messiest. When they are living together they may need to negotiate ground rules regarding household management that are more or less acceptable to both of them.

I have put a typical list of household chores in the appendix to help you create your work plan.

If you find that you are not resolving the division of household tasks, it probably means that something else is causing the problem. Fighting about housework is often a symptom of some other problem—usually one of the three other areas mentioned above. Chores may seem to be the safest thing to fight about. If this is the case, you will need to figure out what else is not working in the relationship and resolve that first.

AREAS THAT REQUIRE SERIOUS ATTENTION

There are some situations that cannot be resolved as a couple and that require a serious commitment to change on an individual's part before the relationship can work:

- extramarital affairs
- addiction to drugs or alcohol
- violence, either physical, sexual or verbal
- *untreated* mental health problem

When any of the above problems exist, they need to be dealt with first. **The affair, addiction or violence must stop, and the mental health problem treated, before a relationship is safe for both partners to commit to each other.**

A FINAL WORD

Many areas of communication have been covered in this book. Making them all work may seem like an overwhelming task. There is absolutely no need to practise all these skills at all times. Making the effort to practise even a few of them will demonstrate that you are committed and you care. As mentioned in the beginning of the book, individuals in couple relationships are very forgiving of each other as long as they feel their mate cares about them, is committed to making the partnership work, and is willing to make small changes in his or her behaviour to accomplish this. When both strive to create this cooperative and loving environment, they will have a rewarding relationship.

APPENDIX

LIST OF HOUSEHOLD RESPONSIBILITIES

CLEANING AND TIDYING
Cleaning kitchen
Cleaning bathroom
Clearing up/dusting living areas
Vacuuming/mopping floor surfaces
Clearing up after meals
Washing dishes or loading and emptying dishwasher
Making beds

MEALS AND GROCERIES
Checking food supplies
Planning menus
Making grocery list
Buying groceries
Cooking food
Replacing kitchen utensils

LAUNDRY
Collecting laundry
Washing laundry
Folding/sorting/putting away clean laundry
Ironing
Dropping off/ picking up dry cleaning
Sewing tears, buttons, etc.

INSIDE MAINTENANCE
Arranging for repairs
Painting jobs
Decorating
Staying at home for servicemen
Carrying out simple household repairs

OUTSIDE MAINTENANCE
Grass cutting
Gardening
Snow removal
Garbage removal
Hanging/taking down Christmas lights

CAR REPAIRS
Car maintenance
Arranging for or performing oil changes
Checking tires
Arranging for rust proofing
Arranging for car repairs

FINANCES
Paying bills
Renewing subscriptions
Sending off insurance claims
Dealing with car insurance, license
Dealing with house insurance
Dealing with life insurance
Organizing savings and investments
Organizing RRSPs

CHILDREN'S ACTIVITIES
Organizing children's time
Supervising children
Discipline
Waking up children
Getting children to bed
Getting children off to school
Supervising children's cleanliness routines
Organizing children's activities
Volunteering for activity fundraisers
Driving for activities
Arranging for daycare
Driving children to/from daycare

Arranging for evening sitters
Meeting teachers
Attending parents' days and evenings
Volunteering for school activities
Organizing money for school trips and books
Signing permission slips
Organizing appropriate clothing for trips
Taking time off for children's illnesses
Taking time off for children's appointments
Organizing summer schedule for children
Buying children's clothing
Buying birthday gifts for children's friends
Organizing birthday parties for children
Buying birthday and other gifts for children and relatives
Sending greeting cards for birthdays and religious holidays

LEISURE TIME

Organizing vacations
Maintaining social links
Entertaining
Preparing for entertainment
Community involvement
Community volunteering

BIBLIOGRAPHY

The two best books that I have read on personality types are:

Briggs Myers, Isabel, and Peter B Myers. *Gifts Differing.* Palo Alto: Consulting Psychologists Press, Inc., 1980.

Kiersey, D., and M. Bates. *Please Understand Me: Character and Personality Types.* Del Mar: Prometheus Nemesis Book Company, 1984.

The two books I lend most often to couples are:

Beck, Aaron T. *Love is Never Enough.* New York: Harper Perennial, 1989.

Hendrix, Harville. *Getting the Love You Want.* New York: Harper Perennial, 1990.

Good books on communication:

Jakubovsky and Lange, *The Assertive Option.* Champaign: Research Press, 1976.

Smith, Manuel, *When I Say No I Feel Guilty.* New York: Bantam, 1975.

Unfortunately both these books are now out of print, but are often to be found in good secondhand bookstores.

Johnson, David. *Reaching Out.* Englewood Cliffs: Prentice Hall, 1972 (nearly thirty years old, but has just been reprinted).

ABOUT THE AUTHOR

When I finished my psychology degree in 1974, I went on to train as a teacher. My goal at that time was to become a child psychologist. Part of that process, in England, was to work in the schools for a few years before graduate school. Those few years became nearly seven as I moved from working in special education, to working with school refusers, and then with delinquent kids. I thoroughly enjoyed working with older teenagers.

When I moved to Canada in 1982, I discovered that I would not be able to continue in this type of work. In the first place, the kind of inner city programmes with which I had been involved did not exist in Ottawa. Secondly, as a new parent I realized that it would be a constant strain to work with this very demanding group of individuals.

At this point a change of career seemed to be called for, and I decided to go back to school and train as a counsellor. While my kids were small and I was working on my master's degree part time, I began leading groups in self-development areas such as assertiveness training, stress management, self-esteem development and, eventually, couples' communication. I finished my master's degree in 1985 and began slowly to build a private practice in counselling.

In 1989, my kids were both in school and I gradually returned to work, taking contracts over the next few years that appealed to my interest in counselling, adult development and the teaching of coping skills. I worked in addictions, mental health and in the prisons, while I built up a private practice.

I now work full time with adults and couples. In January 1994, I became registered with the College of Psychologists of Ontario as part of the new wave of practitioners to be registered at the master's level of education.

I live with my husband Ian and our two children, Ben and Peter, in Carp, Ontario.

Clare Bowles